teach®
yourself

D0268292

how to dj
rob wood

For over 60 years, more than
40 million people have learnt over
750 subjects the **teach yourself**
way, with impressive results.

be where you want to be
with **teach yourself**

For UK order enquiries: please contact Bookpoint Ltd, 130 Milton Park, Abingdon, Oxon OX14 4SB. Telephone: +44 (0) 1235 827720. Fax: +44 (0) 1235 400454. Lines are open 09.00–18.00, Monday to Saturday, with a 24-hour message answering service. Details about our titles and how to order are available at www.teachyourself.co.uk

For USA order enquiries: please contact McGraw-Hill Customer Services, PO Box 545, Blacklick, OH 43004-0545, USA. Telephone: 1-800-722-4726. Fax: 1-614-755-5645.

For Canada order enquiries: please contact McGraw-Hill Ryerson Ltd, 300 Water St, Whitby, Ontario L1N 9B6, Canada. Telephone: 905 430 5000. Fax: 905 430 5020.

Long renowned as the authoritative source for self-guided learning – with more than 40 million copies sold worldwide – the **teach yourself** series includes over 300 titles in the fields of languages, crafts, hobbies, business, computing and education.

British Library Cataloguing in Publication Data: a catalogue record for this title is available from the British Library.

Library of Congress Catalog Card Number: on file.

First published in UK 2005 by Hodder Education, 338 Euston Road, London, NW1 3BH.

First published in US 2005 by Contemporary Books, a Division of the McGraw-Hill Companies, 1 Prudential Plaza, 130 East Randolph Street, Chicago, IL 60601 USA.

This edition published 2005.

The **teach yourself** name is a registered trade mark of Hodder Headline.

Typeset by Transet Limited, Coventry, England.
Printed in Great Britain for Hodder Education, a division of Hodder Headline, 338 Euston Road, London NW1 3BH, by Cox & Wyman Ltd, Reading, Berkshire.

Hodder Headline's policy is to use papers that are natural, renewable and recyclable products and made from wood grown in sustainable forests. The logging and manufacturing processes are expected to conform to the environmental regulations of the country of origin.

Impression number   10 9 8 7 6 5 4 3 2 1
Year   2010 2009 2008 2007 2006 2005

iii

contents

about the author

Since the late '80s Rob Wood has spilt his time between DJing and music journalism. A passionate champion of independent record labels and cutting-edge music, he was deputy editor of dance music magazines *Mixmag Update* and 7, before becoming editor of *Jockey Slut*. He has been a freelance writer covering music, film and travel for magazines and newspapers in the UK and the US. He is currently Head of Content of the ground-breaking music download store TuneTribe.com. As a DJ he has played across the UK and in the US, Norway, France, Spain and Italy as well as at festivals such as The Big Chill, V, Homelands, Bestival, Sonar and the Winter Music Conference. Rob also provides music supervision to a film production company and music/youth consultancy to leading brands. He has compiled the 'vintagegrooves', 'bargrooves: en hiver', and 'Mr and Mrs Smith' compilation albums.

acknowledgements

Thanks to all the DJs who allowed me to pick their brains: Tom Findlay from Groove Armada, Pete Lawrence from The Big Chill, Fred Deakin from Lemon Jelly, Erol Alkan from Trash, Coldcut, Rob da Bank, Miguel Migs, Trevor Nelson, The Glimmers, Craig Richards from Fabric, Yousef, Cosmo, Ewan Pearson, Sandy Rivera, Chris Duckenfield and DJ Format. You are all an inspiration.

Thanks to all those industry bods who helped it happen: Indy Vidyalankara at BBC Radio 1, Sam Pow at The Big Chill, Nick Doherty at Fabric, James Heather at Ninja Tune, Caroline Hoste at Music2Productions, Isabel Guilet at PIAS, Jonas Stone at EPM, Georgia Spencer-Holmes at Helter Skelter, Mark Jackson at Perfecto, Ben Sowton and the Seamless Recordings team.

Big thanks to John Strickland, Ronnie Traynor, Cordelia Plunkett and all the fantastic team at TuneTribe for bearing with me whilst I fretted about deadlines and DJs.

I'm also grateful to music lecturer Ben Carr at Cambridge Regional College for advice on Ableton and Traktor.

I'm particularly indebted to Nick Roden for casting his knowledgeable eyes on my first draft (one of the few people who knows the difference between a stab, a hamster switch and a spelling mistake).

Special thanks for all the expertise and professional guidance from the 'Teach Yourself' team at Hodder Headline especially: Catherine Coe, Lisa Grey, Katie Archer, Louisa Booth and Victoria Roddam.

Loving thanks to my wife Amber for reading various sections of the manuscript whilst knowing it would bore her to tears; for encouraging me through huge workloads; for allowing our home to be a shrine to music; and for putting up with losing me to the book at weekends. I couldn't have done it without you behind me.

This book is dedicated to the DJs in Sheffield who were truly inspiring: Winston Hazel, Parrot and Solid State; and to my parents Sue and Charles as way of explanation of what I have been doing for all these years.

"Without music to decorate it, time is just a bunch of boring production deadlines or dates by which bills must be paid."

Frank Zappa

"One good thing about music, when it hits you, you feel no pain."

Bob Marley

"Those who hear not the music ... think the dancers mad."

Unknown

01

introduction

What is a DJ?

Most people have a pretty good idea of what a disc jockey is. A DJ is someone who plays music to others. Yet a DJ could as much be a person stuck behind a microphone in a hospital playing Top 40 hits, as someone spinning the latest house music to a sea of dancers in a nightclub. Both hospital radio DJs and club DJs are there to entertain people, but in very different ways. Likewise, the techniques used by a hip-hop-mad scratch DJ couldn't be further from that of the mobile disco entertainer DJing at a wedding party.

In fact, DJs are not unlike the Wizard Of Oz. DJs may not work in the Emerald City (although they have been known to appear in nightclubs called Sapphires), yet there are numerous similarities between them and the almighty Oz. The Wizard was a cranky, old man who hid behind a curtain, desperately hellbent on controlling all those around him through mechanical devices and audio tricks. Isn't this what DJs do? Hide behind a mixing console, trying to manipulate people? Luckily, DJing is a lot more fun than being a wizard. Where as the Wizard was able to bring happiness to Dorothy, the Scarecrow, the Tin Man and Cowardly Lion, DJs have it within their grasp to bring joy to many, many more.

The truth is, the humble DJ comes in many forms, some not as humble as others. As a budding DJ you probably already have a good idea of the type of disc jockey you'd like to be. Perhaps you'd like nothing better than to learn how to make great mixes at home or at a friend's party. Maybe you'd like to be that person tucked away in the corner of your local bar playing R'n'B to a packed crowd. Or is it your goal to have your voice drifting across the airwaves of your radio, introducing the new release by Röyksopp or The Roots? Or perhaps you are determined to make a living by playing the music you love to nightclubs full of enthusiastic dancers.

Whatever type of DJ you have ambition to be, this book will help you reach your goal. Whether your taste is hip-hop, house, techno, trance, drum'n'bass, garage, grime, reggae, Latin, afrobeat, bhangra, chillout or whatever, this book sets out to teach you the practical skills you need to become a DJ. From buying the right kind of equipment to mixing to programming to beating nerves, this book intends to give you all the information and insider tips you need to master every aspect of DJing, from learning it at home to being paid to perform professionally.

But where do DJs come from?

The rise of the DJ

DJs have come a long way since the craft began with the advent of radio. The flat disc gramophone may have been invented in the 1880s by Emile Berliner, but it wasn't until the turn of the century when broadcasting became possible that radio and music could be married together. The radio age began in earnest in the 1920s when public service announcements and weather forecasts were scattered among pieces of music on fledgling stations in America and Britain.

Somewhere in the middle of this, sitting between the development of radio advertising and the development of popular music, was the obliging DJ. Likely to be playing jazz, swing or big band music, DJs carved a professional niche for themselves as presenters, salesmen and trendsetters. With the emergence of rhythm and blues in the 1940s and '50s, radio DJs such as Al Benson and Eddie O'Jay became influential heroes. From this black music, rock'n'roll was born with DJ Alan Freed helping push through its delivery.

By the late '50s and throughout the '60s, the DJ was at the heart of the explosion of youth culture and the development of music industry stables such as the Top 40. Up to this point the DJ had been largely a radio-based animal. But increasingly he'd be called upon to replace bands in ballrooms and at dances. The word *discothèque* might have its origins in wartime France, but it was jazz, and later twist clubs, in London and New York, where the DJ found he could earn a meagre living from entertaining people through the uniting power of music.

The Swinging Sixties saw DJs become important attractions in their own right at venues in London such as The Lyceum, and at nights like The Scene and Disneyland. The DJ became key to the development of strange and wonderful new youth subcultures in the UK and the US. Whilst the discovery of psychedelics was fuelling The Summer Of Love on the west coast of America, Britain was beginning a long, continuing love of black music from the US. As the '60s came to a rude halt with the deepening crisis in Vietnam, Northern Soul became established in white working-class towns such as Manchester, Wigan and Blackpool. The scene revolved around DJs such as Ian Levine championing soul records like Gloria Jones' 'Tainted Love'. This was the first real club scene and DJs were the glue that held it together.

The early 1970s also saw the beginnings of the flamboyant disco movement. Emerging from New York, out of the psychedelic soul of Sly and The Family Stone, Motown's Norman Whitfield, and the orchestrated dance music from Gamble and Huff's Philadelphia-based studios, it was a sound developed and taken on by DJs Francis Grasso, Steve D'Acquisto, David Mancuso and Nicky Siano in the black and gay clubs of the Big Apple. Grasso in particular is of note in the evolvement of the slip-cue and beat mixing – techniques which are still used by all DJs today. The DJs who followed these pioneers throughout the life and commercial death of disco, such as New York's Walter Gibbons and Larry Levan, are still a musical inspiration to different generations of music fans, producers and DJs today.

By the late '70s, the DJ's tools where changing with the emergence of the 12" single and the remix. Turntables that allowed DJs to alter the tempo of records became commonplace too. Now DJs were able to segue together dance tracks into one endless soundtrack to long nights of hedonism and at the same time manipulate the music they were playing to better suit the dancefloor.

The impact of this and the music that became known as 'garage' (born out of Levan's Paradise Garage night and Tony Humphries' Zanzibar) quickly went on to be felt further afield. DJs such as Frankie Knuckles took the underground '80s dance sound to the warehouses of Chicago. The Windy City was as central to the development of house music as New York. At the same time as Knuckles was playing Chaka Khan and Eddy Grant songs to Chicago's black gay underclass, Ron Hardy was ripping up the rule book with an astonishing mix of European synthesiser music, mutant disco and tracks made by local musicians who were experimenting with drum machines and samplers.

Out of this melting pot house music was born, championed most notably by Chicago's Trax record label. Almost at the same time the underground music scene of the Motor City of Detroit was coming to life with the sound of techno. Influenced by electronic pioneers Kraftwerk and George Clinton's psychedelic funk outfit Parliament as much as disco, Derrick May, Juan Atkins and DJ Kevin Saunderson began making this strange robotic form of dance music that would go on to be played by DJs around the world.

It wasn't long before the intriguing and cosmic new sounds of house and techno began cropping up in DJs' sets at gay and straight nights in London, Manchester and Sheffield. Soul, rare groove, hip-hop and electro-obsessed DJs like Dave Dorrell, Andy Weatherall, Paul Oakenfold and Terry Farley, and crews like Soul II Soul, began to integrate the new sounds into a burgeoning British club culture.

The acid house explosion of the late '80s was the most significant youth culture movement since punk. It had huge impact on the music and leisure businesses; it changed what we listened to, how we danced, how we dressed and even where we went on holiday.

At the heart of this revolution were bedroom-bound producers making cheap but effective dance music. And right alongside them was, of course, the DJ. In fact, DJs became the focus of dance music magazines and became the central attraction for pulling in wide-eyed punters throughout the '90s. As the decade progressed, the eager clubber was spoilt with an ear-splitting choice of new sub-genres of dance music, be it drum'n'bass, trip-hop, tech-house or happy hardcore. As the music diversified, a premier league of DJs went on to form almost a monopoly on the ever-growing super clubs. These superstar DJs would earn thousands by playing the latest dance anthems to gigantic club crowds.

Despite the bubble bursting as club culture went into the millennium, dance music and DJs continued to thrive either in less decadent surroundings, or around the world where the four/four beat has seemed to become the soundtrack to a million nights out.

Whilst the US and the UK led the world, the small Caribbean island of Jamaica cannot be denied its rightful place in the history of the DJ. It was here in the 1950s that the sound system was born, powered by what were locally known as deejays (toasters) and selectors (DJs). Ska, rocksteady, reggae and later ragga all emerged from this vibrant and home-grown DJ culture. Innovators such as Coxsone Dodd and King Tubby gave rise to many practices and techniques that today's DJs would be familiar with. The acetate disc, the 'dub', the use of echo, the rewind – all have their origins in Kingston and its outlaying towns.

The ghetto-based reggae style of DJing was also to have an important effect on the birth of hip-hop in the ghettos of the Bronx, New York. Like reggae, hip-hop is DJ-made music. It grew out of the competition from organisers of rival block parties to out do one another, as DJ Kool Herc wowed crowds by taking the particularly funky and percussive breaks of old funk records and weaved them together to form new and extended, intoxicating rhythms. Herc's amazing parties and primitive mixing were to inspire Grandmaster Flash into taking DJing to the next level, through developing the manual sampling and looping of records without losing a beat. This was the basis of hip-hop. Backed by his MCs, the Furious Five, rapping became incorporated into the DJ sets. By the time Grand Wizard Theodore had invented scratching, the spectacular energy of hip-hop was soon to burst out of the Bronx into downtown Manhattan and beyond.

Hip-hop or rap music has always been about MCs and rapping, but has always also been about DJs and DJing. Hip-hop developed and morphed through the '80s and '90s to become the biggest-selling genre of music in the world. This DJ-based form of music overtook the predominant US musical genre, country and western, and installed itself into the fabric of almost every youth culture around the globe.

Not bad for a bunch of DJs. The craft has come a long way then.

Why be a DJ now?

So DJs have risen to be major cultural players: entertainers who can command vast fees for performing, or for using their knowledge of the dancefloor in productions and remixes. But DJs are champions not gods. They are champions of good music and there is a need for them now as much as any other time, if not more. As we are bombarded with endless sources of entertainment, consumerism and media, music has become ever present. We hear it everywhere and can take it anywhere. There is so much music that we need help. We need DJs as taste-makers and selectors, to help guide us through the bad stuff towards the light of good music.

And now is a great time to do this. Whereas the likes of DJs Kool Herc, David Mancuso, Larry Levan, Kevin Saunderson and more recently Coldcut, Grooverider, Carl Cox, Jeff Mills or Sasha have developed and expanded the craft, the truth is DJing is probably still only in its adolescence. Today's DJ has a far wider choice of music, and many, many more opportunities to showcase and play it. Even more significantly, digital technology has transformed what the DJ is capable of. As we shall see, the techniques which were once solely at the disposal of the studio-based musician or producer, are now easily accessible for the forward-thinking DJ. The ability to manipulate and radically alter music in accordance with the needs of the dancefloor makes DJing more exciting than ever.

With the vast wealth of incredible old and new music available to every DJ, and the mind-shattering technical options open to them, there has never been a better time for smashing down preconceived ideas about genres, styles or fashions. A DJ's inherent desire to excite and surprise their audience is really now able to be fully released. This makes learning to DJ today a great idea.

Are you a DJ?

Learning to DJ is not unlike learning to drive. It is not a skill that can be simply studied. Committing the *Highway Code* to memory, reading road-safety books and watching videos designed to instruct new drivers how to deal with other road users is of benefit to those new to driving, but it will never compensate for the actual experience of learning on the road.

Likewise, to learn to DJ, you are going to need to put in many hours of practice at home. This book will be a great help in achieving your goal of becoming an accomplished DJ, but you will still need to gain hands-on experience learning the craft.

You will do this at home on your own DJ equipment, but you will also need to take the skills you learn there out to bars and clubs in front of audiences before you gain the real experience required to know how to entertain other people. There will be times when you may find it hard. However, bear in mind that the more you DJ, the better you will become. That is a certainty. Again like driving, you will only improve the more you do it.

In addition to this you will need to spend much time searching for new tunes. This is time-consuming and expensive. The equipment doesn't come cheap either. Yet the payback – successfully entertaining and having people enjoy your music – is priceless.

The one requirement you must have to drive you to put the hours and effort in, is a deeply-embedded passion for music. If you want to DJ for the glory, fame and money you are doing it for the wrong reasons. For a start, most DJs make a reasonable, not fantastic, living from their trade. It is only the top 5 per cent of DJs who command mammoth incomes.

In reality DJing is full of late nights, hard work and a lot of travel. To do it you must be committed to the lifestyle and the music. DJing has rarely been about playing someone else's records for easy money. DJs are actually highly-skilled entertainers who spend much of their time looking for music and watching, listening to and befriending other DJs.

This book will help you realise your burning ambition. It will enable you to cut it in terms of mixing with a number of different formats. It will not only tell you which equipment you are going to need, but also take you through the learning process step by step. What's more, it will show you how to become a DJ whose sets work on the dancefloor through effective music programming with a coherent structure. It will give you a thorough understanding of what makes a dancefloor respond. Having mastered these essential skills, the book gives you tips on getting booked as well as a host of useful contacts and information.

In other words, this book provides you with everything you need to know about taking your passion for music to others. I hope you enjoy the ride.

02

tools of the trade

The equipment that any budding DJ needs to master is thankfully relatively easy to use. What's more, as a DJ you do not need to know how it works. It is far more important to know what it does. You don't need to understand what's going on inside the box of tricks but you do need to be able to do tricks with the box!

There are numerous models and brands of the same piece of kit that basically all try to do the same thing with differing amounts of success. It would be pointless to endlessly go through each product on the market when magazines such as *DJ* and *iDJ* run reviews on new models all the time. Instead, we will concentrate on what kit is needed, what it does and give a few recommendations on products that are considered to be very DJ-friendly.

It is also worth remembering that ploughing through the indecipherable user manual of any new electronic gadget can be intimidating at first, but any piece of kit is there to be mastered and used as a tool in your quest to make people jump about in excitement. Don't let the technology dominate you. Let it know who's boss. It is, after all, just a load of souped-up hi-fi at the end of the day.

Vinyl v CD v MP3

First though, you must decide what format of music you will be using. There are three types of formats that DJs use: vinyl – the black round discs; CDs – the smaller silver discs; and MP3 data files.

- Vinyl, otherwise known as records, is made up of tiny circular grooves. The grooves make the record player's needle vibrate. These vibrations are turned into electronic signals that are transformed into the sound that you hear.
- CDs are discs that store music in digital form. One disc can hold 74 minutes of music.
- MP3s are a common type of digital audio file. A piece of music is coded and then compressed into these files to allow computers to store lots of music.

This much you probably know already. But what are the advantages of using one format over another and which kind should you be using?

Vinyl

Despite the ever-increasing switch to CD and MP3 players, the majority of DJs still prefer good old-fashioned vinyl. The reason for this is quite simple. Most DJs have built up large vinyl collections and unsurprisingly want to use it, but more importantly it is the grooves on records that mean those black shiny discs will always be close to a jock's heart.

By its very nature, vinyl, unlike CDs or MP3s, can be 'read'. Firstly, it's easy to tell where you are in a track by seeing how far through the record the needle is. This is helpful for DJs because it lets them know if the record is about to finish and they need to mix in the next track. Or it can let the DJ know that there is plenty of the song playing left so he or she has time to quickly make that all-important dash to the gents or ladies.

An experienced DJ can read the grooves even further. Knowing his or her records well, they will be able to quickly see exactly what section of the track they are at and know what is coming next, which is crucial to expert mixing. Furthermore, because the density of the grooves changes with the structure of every track, a DJ can see where the music is about to change. If you look at any 12" dance single, you will notice that different bands of grooves catch the light in different ways. These are different sections of the track such as the breakdowns and drum parts. Looking at these and getting to know them helps DJs build a mental map of the music.

Added to this is the ability to manipulate vinyl (see Chapter 03: 'Vinyl manipulation'). You can get your hands on it whilst it is playing. You can stop it, push it, scratch it and even throw it into the crowd after a particularly impressive build-up (although this last action is not recommended). Try doing that to an MP3 file.

This ability to get 'hands on' with vinyl makes it very useable. DJs can control vinyl to make the music do what they want. In fact, vinyl is the only format of music that can be directly touched when it is playing. This makes vinyl unique and close to the hearts of many DJs.

CDs

Vinyl does have disadvantages too, though: the main one being its weight. Anyone who has moved house and carried boxes of records up flights of stairs will know how heavy vinyl is.

Lugging a bag full of vinyl between gigs is in fact guaranteed to bring on the curse of the DJ – 'DJ's back' – medically defined as 'a nagging pain inflicted on the lower vertebrae by 12" overload'. The relatively recent invention of record bags and boxes on wheels has been a minor revolution for the working DJ, in equal parts infuriating osteopaths and delighting record box-carrying friends. Notice how famous DJs no longer walk with pronounced stoops. A record bag or box with wheels and collapsible handle is indeed a good investment for any vinyl-carrying DJ.

CDs on the other hand are far easier to carry. CD DJs are best off ditching the unnecessary packaging and placing their collection in a CD carrier case (remember to keep the sleeves for track reference).

But can DJs get 'hands on' with CDs like they can with vinyl? As CD players develop, the discs can be increasingly manipulated in a hands-on way which, when added to portability, is making them increasingly attractive to DJs. These days it is not an uncommon sight to see established DJs unloading their entire vinyl collections on to the poor staff of second-hand record shops in an attempt to free themselves of the burden of carrying them whilst giving in to the demands of their partners who want to reclaim their living room floor space. Beware: a record collection can take over your home if it is consistently well fed.

Any DJ ditching their vinyl will have either transferred their prized collection on to CD or converted it into MP3 files. The fact that CDs are 'burnable' is another major advantage. Music can be downloaded from across the globe and copied on to a CD-R ready to be played out in minutes. In other words, CDs can now be used like vinyl, plus they can be cheaper, are easier to carry and you can record on to them.

MP3 and digital audio files

MP3s are compressed digital files of audio data. There are other formats such as WMA, WAV, AIFF, MOD, AAC, FLAC and MP4, but MP3 is the most widespread format. WAV and AIFF are uncompressed audio files that are used in recording studios.

MP3s are loved for the fact that they can be swapped and sourced so easily. Because they are digital they take up no physical storage space, only hard drive space. What's more, because they are compressed, they take up very little virtual space too, so a computer can store many of these files. On paper it would seem to be the perfect format.

However, there is a sound quality issue with MP3s. All formats of vinyl, CD and MP3 sound different, but digital files have been accused of sounding flatter than CDs because certain frequencies have been left out. However, high-quality, DJ-friendly downloads are now available from sites such as TuneTribe.com and ClickGroove.com.

It is also worth noting that although you can easily scan lists of digital files on a laptop, you can't flick through them in the same way that you can with records or CDs. In the middle of a set, a good DJ will be regularly flicking through their box making mental notes about which songs would work with others. The ability to handle these formats helps with set programming. But it is easy to create lists with the latest MP3 software so you can remind yourself which tracks work well together. You can keep songs that go well together or are in the same genre or are of a similar tempo, in groups.

Overall, MP3 technology is the most exciting development in DJ culture in recent years. Not only can thousands of songs be stored on a single laptop, cue points can be pre-saved, beat mixing is made easier as MP3 mixing software can calculate the correct speed for the next record, and live editing of tracks is now fully in the grasp of DJs.

Many DJs would tell you not to ignore vinyl for the sake of being modern. It is the format that gave birth to DJ culture after all. The truth is no one format is better than another. There are numerous advantages and disadvantages with each and they all sound different to boot. You need to choose which is going to be easiest for you to use, i.e. the format that you are most comfortable with. Or, more cleverly, use a combination of formats to give you access to the widest choice of music possible. In fact, more and more DJs are using multiple formats so that they have as much music at their disposal as possible. And it is the music that matters. Without the right music, all the technology in the world won't save you.

Turntables

DJing was born out of the use of turntables. The wheels of steel are a DJ's best friend. Watch a DJ work and you'll notice how they are finely tuned into the way their turntables operate. Such turntables are not dissimilar to your home hi-fi's record player, but they have been specially adapted to give the DJ greater control over their music. Controlling the music is crucial for DJing. Some record players made for DJs are better at this than others.

The first point to look for is how the turntable is powered. If it is belt-driven, it is rotated via a rubber band. This gives you very inaccurate control over the turntable. Instead look to buy direct-drive turntables. These are operated by a strong motor which allows you to almost instantly stop and start records. Direct drives will also spin the turntables at constant speeds which again makes mixing so much easier.

Technics SL1200/SL1210s

If you are going to be using vinyl it is worth spending as much as you can afford on a decent pair of direct-drive decks. Learning to mix on cheap decks, or worse still belt-driven decks, will be harder and will only cause you problems if you get to play at club level. The question is: which decks? And the answer is easy. Technics. They are the industry standard. Ninety-nine per cent of clubs and bars use Technics SL1200 turntables. This means that by learning to mix on Technics you will feel at home DJing in most venues.

Introduced in 1972 Technics turntables revolutionised what the DJ is capable of by providing far more control over the music. The SL1200 and 1210 (a black version of the same model) are beautiful, highly effective machines. They are strong and sturdy with a motor that provides excellent torque (turning power). This means they can be knocked around by scratching DJs, work perfectly through endless sets and start, stop and speed up exactly when you want them to.

If you can afford them at around £500 a pair, buy them. They are less fiddly and better made than the competition. What's more, because they are so well built they keep their value on resale. Indeed, their indestructibility means that buying a second-hand pair is not a bad idea.

The fact that they are prevalent in clubs across the world means that if you learn on Technics at home, you shouldn't struggle to use the turntables elsewhere. The only design fault with these turntables is that the pitch control isn't stable when it's close to zero. The new Mk V version has solved the problem completely and comes with some useful extra features too. Expect to pay just over £600 for a pair.

figure 1 the Technics SL1210 Mk V turntable
source: Panasonic UK

If you don't buy Technics you need to know what strengths and weaknesses to look for:

1 Don't buy belt-driven turntables. They use a rubber band to rotate the platter which means you have far less control. Records will jump from one speed to another at the tiniest touch – disastrous for expert mixing. Only get direct-drive turntables – these give the platter a consistent and manageable speed.

2 Reliable pitch control is essential. The varispeed controller should be consistent, precise and smooth.

3 A strong motor for decent torque is crucial. This dictates the power of the platter's spin.

4 The turntable must be sturdy. You want a heavy weight shell that houses an unshakeable platter that doesn't wobble. This will help keep the needle on the record.

5 The best decks have electromagnetic brakes for quicker platter stopping.

Gemini, Vestax and Numark all make good top-of-the-range models but despite welcome gadgets such as straight tone arms for better scratching, it is worth spending that little bit more for Technics. If money is scarce you are best advised to get a second-hand pair of Technics rather than cheap decks that don't do what you need them to. (See Appendix 1, page 171, for descriptions of turntable features.)

CD decks

Thankfully the double console CD decks that most clubs had in the '90s are being replaced by the far superior stand-alone CD units. The double consoles were hard to use and lacked precision. The modern stand-alone CD deck such as Pioneer CDJ-800 (costs around £360) or the Pioneer CDJ-1000 Mk2 (around £580) are excellent machines that allow you to cue up any point in the track, change the pitch and do nearly everything that you can with a turntable as well as some useful tricks such as creating loops. Some will even beatmatch for you, albeit in a rudimentary way. Other models such as Technics SLDZ1200 now have a

figure 2 the Pioneer CDJ-1000 Mk2 CD deck
source: Pioneer GB Ltd

spinning platter or virtual record built into the top of the deck that allows full hands-on manipulation of the CD to the extent where you can even scratch. You can also use MP3s (see page 22 'MP3 software, hardware, Final Scratch and Ableton Live').

The best advice is to buy single CD units so you can plug them into a mixer and use them alongside turntables, although this is expensive. The Pioneer CDJ-1000 Mk2 is rapidly becoming the industry standard much like the Technics SL1200, although the reliable Denon DN 1800F is fairly commonplace too. These are expensive so you might be better off using the well-made Pioneer CDJ-800s instead which are a good alternative. It is important to get your hands on the CD deck you are interested in and have a go with it before you buy. Make sure it has a jog wheel and a fast start button. (See Appendix 2, page 173 for descriptions of CD deck features.)

Mixers

The music from your two decks needs to be mixed together and this is where mixers come into the equation. Mixers basically take the music from two or more sources and allow the DJ to merge them together. At the same time the DJ can monitor the music on headphones. This means you can listen to a track whilst another is playing. This is crucial to mixing because you need to work out exactly which part of the next track you are going to use.

Different styles of DJing have different requirements of their mixer. It is important to understand this before you buy a mixer. DJs who beatmatch – such as house or techno DJs – use mixers to blend tracks together, whilst hip-hop DJs – sometimes referred to as turntablists – use mixers to perform their scratching techniques. This means beatmatching DJs are less rough on the crossfader and make more use of EQ channels, whilst turntablists batter the crossfader and need to be able to alter how it operates, such as reversing the fade to perform certain moves using the infamous 'hamster switch'. If you are going to be playing mainly hip-hop music look for a mixer with turntablist-friendly features. It's a good idea to make sure you can replace the crossfader once it is worn out too. If you will be beatmatching it helps to have separate three-band EQ controls for each channel. Being able to control the EQ channels will improve your sound and mixing.

The good news is that you can learn to mix on cheap mixers. As long as they have basic controls and the right inputs and outputs for your equipment, they will do. More expensive models, such as the fantastic Allen & Heath mixers, will have superior sound quality and extra features. These extra features can be useful. Kill switches for instance allow you to cut out certain parts of the music which can be used to dramatic effect. BPM (beats per minute) counters, however, are a waste of time. These supposedly help you match the beats and tempo of two different records by displaying each BPM. Your ears are a far more effective and fine tuned instrument for measuring how fast a beat is going, so ignore these counters.

When buying a mixer do check that the sound is good and that the headphone output is loud so you can hear what you are doing when playing on a loud sound system. You might want to purchase one that includes sound effects such as the Pioneer DJM-500 mixer (around £400). This isn't essential but is a nice luxury if you can afford it. If you can't afford it don't worry, you can always buy a separate FX unit as your skills progress. See Chapter 04 'FX' for more information about buying FX units. (See also Appendix 3, page 175, for an explanation of mixer features.)

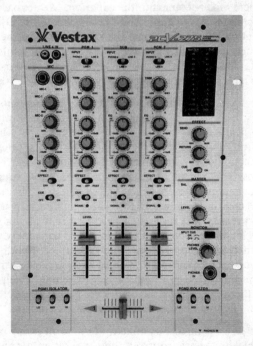

figure 3 the Vestax PCV-275 DJ mixer
source: Vestax Corporation of Japan/Vestax Europe

Headphones

All DJs need a decent pair of headphones to help them cue up records. Headphones, or 'cans' as they are sometimes referred to, let the DJ listen to the next bit of music they want to play, helping find the right part of the track and working out the right tempo.

Cheap headphones are likely to let you down. The sound quality may be sufficient to mix with at home, but in a working environment you are unlikely to be able to hear music clearly enough against the noise levels of a club's sound system. Cheap headphones when battered about by a working DJ will often snap around the head rest. The lead could also develop a faulty connection when yanked around and could therefore let you down at a crucial moment.

It is thus good advice to buy a more expensive pair that are designed for DJ use. These will cost between £50 and £150. Make sure they have a long, durable lead, are lightweight and well padded around the ears. They must be loud and clear, cutting out as much background noise as possible. Avoid headphones that have leads which get easily intertwined. These are likely to get wrapped around your neck and be annoying.

Slipmats

The cheapest and most unassuming piece of kit you need is the humble slipmat. Chuck out the rubber mats that your turntables came with and get a pair of slipmats which should not set you back more than a tenner.

A slipmat is a round felt mat that sits between the vinyl and the platter. It is used to stop the friction between the record and the platter interfering with a DJ's manoeuvres. In other words it lets the platter rotate, or 'slip', beneath whilst a DJ holds the record still. Without slipmats a DJ would not be able to get hands on with vinyl and therefore would not have control of the music. Avoid over embellished designs on slipmats as the print will make them less slippery.

If you turn up at a gig and there are no slipmats, all is not lost though. Take a record's plastic inner sleeve and punch a hole through the middle for the turntable's spindle. This should give you enough 'slip' for the time being.

figure 4 slipmat on Technics turntable
source: Nicky J. Sims/Redferns

Cartridges and needles

A needle, otherwise known as a 'stylus', is a sharp piece of synthetic diamond that slots into a record's grooves reading the minute bumps within. The cartridge transforms these vibrations into an electronic signal that becomes the music.

New needles can be bought to replace worn-out ones. This is cheaper than replacing the whole cartridge. Needles will be about £20–£30. A basic pair of cartridges (such as Stanton 500Als) will be around £50 whilst the best for DJing will be about £150.

There are two types of cartridge. The more commonplace ones screw into the underside of the tone arm's headshell. They are then connected to four small colour-coded copper wires. These tend to be better for the knocking about scratching DJs will give them. All-in-one cartridges screw straight into the tone arm and have superior sound quality. Their slimline shape also allows the DJ to see better where the needle is and they track better, i.e. they are less likely to jump.

figure 5 headshell and cartridge
source: Numark Alesis Europe Ltd

figure 6 an all-in-one cartridge
source: Numark Alesis Europe Ltd

MP3 software, hardware, Final Scratch and Ableton Live

If you have your heart set on DJing with MP3s you will need a computer with lots of memory and software that allows you to listen to them, such as RealPlayer, Media Player and WinAmp for PCs, and RealPlayer, QuickTime and iTunes for Mac.

You can then either burn the files on to CD and use CD decks to mix them or use mixing software on your computer. Such software comes in many shapes and forms with most of it being fairly easy to use. PCDJ, DJ Mix Station and Virtual Turntables can all be recommended. The PCDJ software can be used with Numark's DMC-1 which is effectively a CD 'deck-like' dual controller for mixing MP3s. These are now a little out of date but can still be purchased for around £200.

Native Instruments' Traktor DJ Mixer is another piece of software which enables mouse-controlled (i.e. laptop) interaction with MP3 and other files. It is pretty impressive, although remains slightly fiddly. It allows you to see tracks playing in graphic waveform which is great for clearly visualising upcoming sections of music and for chopping and looping bits of tracks. It has EQ, kill switches, beat counters and automatic beat alignment which makes mixing easy. It even has filters and pre-set scratches. Traktor DJ Mixer can only be used on PCs. The improved Traktor DJ Studio 2.6 is designed for live mixing, remixing and mix recording with MP3, WAV, AIFF and audio CDs, and can be used with Apple Mac operating systems as well as PC. It is also compatible with Final Scratch 2.0. The price is around £130. Native Instruments have also developed a piece of hardware which has a double deck panel to run alongside Traktor called the Hercules DJ Console. This costs in the region of £170.

For those who want to be more hands on, the CDN95 Dual MP3/CD Player is Numark's flagship MP3 player. It allows you to swap between CD and MP3 formats. You can also scratch using MP3 files. This gives you real flexibility using different formats but doesn't come cheap. Expect to pay over £400.

figure 7 Numark's CDN95 dual MP3/CD player
source: Numark Alesis Europe Ltd

One new piece of kit that is winning fans aplenty is the Technics
SL-DZ1200. This is the first direct-drive digital turntable. It
looks, and more importantly, feels like spinning vinyl on the
classic Technics 1200 turntable. The slip surface of the 10"
platter allows you to spin, scratch and manipulate tracks in a
number of formats including CD, MP3 and AAC (AAC is the
digital file format iTunes offers). Along with its realistic vinyl
feel, the SL-DZ1200 lets you store, play back, scratch and loop
sampled media from a removable memory card. You can also
trigger up to six samples in real time allowing you add spice to
your sets. At around £575, these amazing machines are
expensive though.

figure 8 the Technics SL-DZ1200 digital turntable
source: Panasonic UK

Final Scratch

Better still are pieces of hardware that allow you to mix MP3s on turntables such as the Soundgraph D-Vinyl2020. The biggest recent breakthrough development, in DJ equipment terms, however, is Stanton's Final Scratch system. It's so clever that it's hard to believe it's true. It effectively allows the modern DJ to combine the benefits of digital technology with the analogue control that DJs love. In other words it enables a DJ to carry thousands of tracks to a gig stored on a computer and then play them on turntables as if they were records.

Using a special unit to interface between the MP3s on a laptop and normal record decks, it uses custom made pieces of 'vinyl' to feed a time-code back to the computer, enabling it to work out how fast and in which direction the turntables are moving. You can speed up, slow down and scratch an MP3 by manhandling the 'vinyl'. You can even cue by picking up the needle and going to another part of the track. You will never need to carry a box of records to another gig, but yet will have your entire collection with you as if on vinyl. Incredible!

figure 9 Stanton Final Scratch kit with CD deck, mixer and turntable
source: Stanton

Some clubs are cottoning on to this fast by installing Final Scratch's ScratchAmps in DJ booths so DJs only need bring their laptop and Final Scratch records. You'll see and hear DJs such as Roni Size using this great piece of kit.

As well as being compatible with analogue turntables, Final Scratch 2.0 allows CD DJs to use specially made CDs to mix with on CD players.

Final Scratch 2.0 can be used on PCs and Macs, and retails at around £530.

Ableton Live

The boundary between studio and DJ technology is increasingly blurred. No more is this evident than with the adoption of Ableton Live. Ableton Live is a software package for studio sequencing which many DJs are falling in love with.

Designed by Germans Robert Henke and Gerhard Behles from the experimental electronic band Monolake, it brings DJing and production together. Essentially it is a very clever sequencer with DJ tools. It allows full MIDI interface between studio or DJ equipment. You can remix or combine many different types of music files such as MP3 (only with the latest version), WAV, AIFF or FLAC on both Mac and PC. Its design is brilliantly intuitive, making it surprisingly easy to use.

This software enables DJs to re-edit or remix tracks and chop them up into different sections. This is one of the reasons why it has never been so easy to play your own musical creations or re-edits of other people's productions whilst DJing. This can really help make your sets stand out from other DJs.

On top of this, as its name suggests, Ableton Live is designed to be used with audiences in a live setting as well as in a studio recording environment. It makes mixing different styles of music very easy. As if by magic you can warp different tempos and pitches enabling you to place supposedly impossible-to-mix songs together. It also has numerous FX and instruments which you can add into the mix.

figure 10 Ableton Live
source: Ableton

To use Live to keep songs in time with any others you want to play, you need to place warp markers into the digital audio file to indicate the location of the track's beats. Once warp markers are in the right place, Live will know how to match songs of any tempo without the dreaded squealing voices on vocal tracks. With the ability to time-align audio files, many DJs are incorporating songs into their sets that weren't recorded at a steady tempo. Music from bands such as Led Zeppelin or The Beatles, for example, can be warp marked to the point that they will play back perfectly alongside a rigid dance beat. This amazing development opens up music to DJs that they never could have beat matched before.

DJs such as JD Twitch and JG Wilkes from Optimo in Glasgow have used this software to great effect, mixing up a heady brew of techno, disco, pop and punk all in a seamless mix which would have been impossible less than ten years ago. DJ Sasha uses it too, as does breakbeat DJ Rennie Pilgrem and dance act Underworld.

There are a number of different versions of Ableton Live. Ableton Live 4 has won a number of awards for being an excellent DJ tool. (Note that you cannot use MP3 files with Ableton Live 4 as it cannot use compressed audio files.) If ripping tracks from a CD, make sure your iTunes (or other ripping programme) is set to rip in either AIFF or WAV formats. Ableton Live 4 costs around £240.

At the time of going to print, Ableton Live 5 is just coming out of beta testing and is available to pre-order. Compressed files such as MP3s can be used for the first time with Ableton 5. In addition, Live 5 will automatically analyse songs for tempo information and create the appropriate warp markers, making it an even more DJ-friendly programme.

DJs wishing to use Traktor, Ableton or digital music files generally will obviously need a laptop to operate and to store files on that they can take to gigs. You will need a sound card with outputs that can interface with a club mixer. It is also a good idea to use a hard drive as if it were a virtual record box. A big hard drive (maybe even two) is a good thing to have. It will hold more information than a standard laptop which is a definite necessity if you are using Ableton 4 as it uses AIFF and WAV files which are not compressed and therefore take up a lot of memory. Using a hard drive also helps keep all your digital music in one place, rather than on your desktop at home and laptop for gigs. It can thus be used as a virtual storage case, and alongside your laptop and sound card, meaning you have the self-contained and very portable kit needed for digital mixing.

By making use of Ableton Live and Traktor's MIDI interface, you could also incorporate a MIDI controller for more hands-on digital DJing. You can purchase a MIDI controller for anywhere between £50–£400. With one of these you can assign full control of your digital files to the controller. This allows you to be more hands on than using a mouse or keyboard. You would be able to crossfade, EQ and add effects from the control box.

Technology is thus making the DJ's kit more complicated but opening up new, exciting possibilities all the time as well as saving a lot of vinyl-induced backache. Whichever type of hardware or software you are interested in buying though, make sure you see it demonstrated in the shop and have a go yourself to see how it feels. Better still, if buying software, go to the developers' website and download a free demo of the programme you are interested in so that you get a real feel for it and can decide if it's what you want. You can do this, for instance, for Native Instruments' Traktor (www.nativeinstruments.de) and Ableton (www.ableton.com) programmes.

DJing with iPods

The all-conquering march of Apple's iPod across the market for personal MP3 players looks set to continue for a while yet. It has even crept into the world of DJing with bars letting customers bring their iPods and play their favourite tunes. People have been doing a primitive form of DJing using these devices. This is fine for bars and undoubtedly fun allowing people to unleash their tastes on others.

However much of an iPod enthusiast you are though, don't for a second think you can DJ professionally with these machines. The sound quality and lack of control are way below the standard needed for DJing.

Gadgets that enhance the iPod's usability such as Numark's iDJ Mixing Console allow two iPods to be mixed using a two-channel mixer complete with headphone and microphone sockets and a three-band EQ. This is great for iPod-mad novice DJs who have no intention of learning to mix, and perhaps a true innovation for mobile DJs, but not to be touched by club DJs. With no pitch control you will not be able to beat match. Without beat matching you won't be playing many clubs.

Your mission is to rock dancefloors, and the iPod, whilst great for listening to music on the move, will not help you achieve this.

03 mixing

There is good news and bad news when it comes to learning to mix. The good news is once you get the hang of it, like riding a bike, it will stay with you forever. The bad news is, again like riding a bike, it takes a while and you need to put the hours in practising. To start with you will be a bit wobbly, but you will improve and get better and better as you add techniques and refine your sense of the mix. But at least you won't suffer from a sore behind.

The bulk of this chapter explains how to mix records together. You need to read this even if you intend to mix only with CDs or MP3s because it sets out the basic principles of mixing two pieces of music together.

First you must understand the typical structure of dance music. To be able to weave elements of two pieces of music together, you must be able to spot those elements and know how they interact in the first place.

Track structure: beats, bars and phrases

To able to beat mix you must be able to distinguish the separate elements that make up a track and then understand how they work together to give each track a structure and feel.

Thankfully most dance music has the same basic rhythmic feel. It has a 1, 2, 3, 4 pulse. In a house record you can hear the kick drum beating this rhythm out. In hip-hop and most funk records the kick drum hits on the first of these four rhythmic pulses (often known as the downbeat). The same 1, 2, 3, 4 pulse structure is also present in drum'n'bass, R'n'B, techno, trance and most other dance styles apart from reggae and jazz.

Each group of 1, 2, 3, 4 pulses or beats is known as a bar. Bars in rock and reggae are often made up of different numbers of beats depending on the rhythmic mood of the song. In most dance music though each bar is almost always four beats long. This makes it easy to dance to and, better still, easy to mix.

Try listening to some of your tunes carefully. See if you can make out the bars by counting the beats. Doing this gives you a sense of the rhythm and structure of a track. But as you will notice there is more going on in each bar than just the kick drum. You will usually hear a number of other drums, cymbals and percussion. It is useful to be able to differentiate between these different sounds.

A snare drum is often used to make the rhythm more complex. It has a tight but tinny 'thwack' sound that often marks the off-beat between the kick drum's thuds.

Likewise hi-hats can mark the off-beat too. Hi-hats are the sound of two cymbals opening and closing together. 'Open' hi-hats make a 'pss-soup' type sound and fall halfway between each beat of the kick drum. 'Closed' hi-hats make a 'tiss, tiss' sound as they quickly close together. Hi-hats help make the rhythm busier by dividing up the bars further so they aren't just a collection of 1, 2, 3, 4 beats.

To summarise so far, the basic rhythmic structure of a dance track can be divided up like this:

- The closed hi-hat is the tiny, high-pitched 'tiss, tiss' running quickly through the track.
- The open hi-hat is the slower high-pitched 'pss-soup' sound.
- The snare drum is the loud 'thwack'.
- The kick drum (or bass drum) is the low-pitched 'boom'.

It is important that you can distinguish between these separate elements because it will help you discriminate between the percussion and beats of two different tunes which is crucial to beat mixing. If you have EQ controls on your mixer, you can use them to help you hear the different instruments. For instance, you can turn down the treble and mid-range EQs. This will highlight the bass end of a track, making the kick drum more pronounced.

At this stage it is useful to also point out that bars are regularly grouped together into 'phrases'. These are the building blocks of the structure of each track. A phrase is often four bars long. As we've seen, there are four beats to the bar (also known as '4/4 time'). Likewise, music is often arranged into four- or eight-bar phrases. It's a good idea to train yourself to be able to hear the phrases as well as the beats and bars as dance music is constructed from these. New things happen in the music after phrases and it is an advantage to be able to predict this.

There will often be a musical marker at the end of each phrase. There might be an extra drum or percussion sound after every four bars and a cymbal after every eight bars. These help to punctuate the music and hearing them gives you a signal that a new musical element is about to be introduced.

The length of a phrase varies depending on the genre to some extent. R'n'B, hip-hop, funk and disco will have four bars in phrases, whilst house, techno and trance will have eight.

Drum'n'bass, grime and UK garage tends to vary, jumping between four- and eight-bar phrases.

As you will no doubt hear, each record has more going on than basic rhythm parts though. It would certainly be a dull tune that had only drums and cymbals in it. There will often be other percussion for a start. This could be the 'slappety-slap' sound of the bongos, the roll of the tom-toms, the clank of a cow bell or the clap of a hand clap. These all add to the dynamism of the rhythm and will be sure to get your audience moving.

Another important element for dance music is of course the bass line. This is the huge, deep sound that, when heard in a club, makes the chips you have just eaten in your stomach rumble. The bass line works in tandem with the drums to make a groove – an infectious repetitive rhythm that makes people dance in different ways depending on how athletic they are. For a classic example of how the drums and bass line work up a groove together listen to practically any James Brown record. The groove is what makes things funky and the bass line is essential to this. Mr Brown certainly knew a thing or two about grooves.

Tracks will have melody too. This could be provided by a variety of different instruments (horns, saxophone, guitar, organ, keyboard, strings) or even a sample. The melody is the bit that sticks in your head. It gives the tune its identity. In fact it's usually the part you see people humming as they walk along listening to their iPod oblivious to the world around them.

The other key element to a track is, of course, the vocals. The vocals are what makes a tune a song. The words add emotional meaning but also act as another kind of melody. Not all tracks will have a person singing or rapping on them but many will.

Now listen to a record and see if you can pick out all these separate elements. Learn how they fit into different bars and phrases.

Vinyl manipulation

Getting hands on with vinyl is a beautiful thing. You need to learn how to caress the vinyl so it does what you want. You must treat it with respect so that you don't damage the recording and you also have to make sure you don't knock the needle off when it's playing which is perhaps the most embarrassing thing that can happen to a DJ. There is nothing worse than 300 clubbers turning round to look at you with hate in their eyes as you sheepishly put the needle back on the record. Don't worry if you do this once in a while though – all DJs make this mistake occasionally.

Making sure you don't damage the vinyl is easy. Simply don't scratch the grooves with the needle. It's easy to mark the record by 'grazing' it alongside anything hard or sharp. Damaging it this way causes crackles, pops and scratches in the sound. Therefore keep the vinyl in its protective sleeve when you are not using it and avoid using it as a frisbee or ashtray.

Similarly, make sure you don't knock the needle when a record is playing. It is not hard to do this. Don't be clumsy and knock the deck about. It's there to be manipulated as a tool, not chucked around like a bag of spanners. Make sure your shirt sleeve does not catch the tone arm or cartridge.

Learning to manipulate vinyl takes a bit more practise. When touching a record, avoid the area near the tone arm (in case you knock the tone arm) and instead touch the opposite edge. You can also be hands on with the central part where the label is.

figure 11 handling the side of a record

figure 12 touching a record's label in the centre

Furthermore, with Technics turntables you should always make sure your left arm or sleeve doesn't accidentally brush past the power switch turning it off. It is surprisingly easy to do.

Now you are ready to practise getting used to the movement of the vinyl.

Practice

1 Find a record that starts with a kick drum (one that you don't like much is best as you may damage it).
2 Turn the power on and put the needle on the record.
3 Get used to placing the needle on the record carefully without using the cueing lever.
4 Get used to starting and stopping the record using the start/stop button.
5 Hold the record still with your hand whilst the platter moves beneath.

6 Practise stopping the record by hand, whilst letting ̶
  spin beneath.
7 Wind the record backwards and forwards with your ̶
8 Practise finding the first beat by winding the record fo ̶
  and backwards.

Cueing up

Cueing up is not something you do in Sainsbury's, cueing up is the practice of getting the needle to the right place, i.e. where you want it on the record. It's best to start practising this by finding the first beat of a record.

Finding the first beat

It's important to be able to find the first beat of a record fast. The easiest way to do this is to let it play and stop it with your hand just after you hear the first beat. You should be using the pads on your fingertips to stop the record. Your fingertips should be on the surface of the record opposite the tone arm. Your slipmat allows the platter to spin beneath whilst you hold the record still. This is the slipmat's sole purpose in life.

To move a record forwards or backwards you need to put your fingers on to the label of the record. Try to learn to do this with one hand so that the other is free for the mixer. Now simply wind the record clockwise or anticlockwise with your forefinger or index finger. When going backwards don't do this too hard – you don't want the platter to stop. When winding forwards, do press hard as you want to cancel the effect of the slipmat. As you wind it backwards you will hear the track play in reverse, and likewise when you move it forward you will hear it speed up and human voices will start to resemble excited mice.

Cueing up on the headphones

Cueing also refers to how DJs listen to two records at once. Using the cueing buttons/switches on the mixer, you can hear the record playing in the room but also the next record being 'cued up' in the headphones. This lets you get the next record ready to be mixed in without anyone else hearing it.

Practice

1 Get a record going on both turntables. Move your crossfader so one is playing out of the speakers and the other isn't.

2 Use the cueing button/switch for the channel that is not coming out of the speakers, and on your headphones you will be able to hear the record that isn't playing to the room.

3 Play with the cueing switches for both channels and see how you can hear both records.

4 Cue back to the record only you can hear. Now move your headphones so that they rest over only one ear. You see DJs do this a lot. It allows you to hear two records at once. You can hear one playing to the room in one ear, and the one being cued up in the other ear.

5 The beats won't be syncopated and therefore the two pieces of music together will sound confusing and a bit of a racket. But see if you can separate the two tracks in your head. DJs need to get used to hearing multiple sources of sound. You must be able to differentiate between them.

Monitors

Monitors are pairs of speakers or a single speaker placed next to the decks that help the DJ hear the music being played to the room over the main PA. This helps you fine tune mixes because in large rooms if the speakers aren't near the DJ booth there will be a slight delay in the sound reaching the DJ's ears. Mixing in this situation is difficult and your mixing can be slightly out due to the sound delay.

With a monitor though, this won't happen. Nearly all clubs will have monitors for the DJs, but some smaller venues such as bars may not.

Split-cueing

Some mixers have a split-cue switch which splits the music into each ear of your headphones. You can therefore hear both records at once without taking the headphones off. This is particularly useful if there isn't a monitor or if the monitor is broken.

Slip-cueing

Slip-cueing is the act of starting a record off right on the beat. You need to practise this. Being able to start a record off the right beat, at the right speed, from the moment you release it, is crucial. You will need to do this with every mix.

Practice

1 Find a record that starts with a kick drum.
2 Find the first beat and hold the record still.
3 Move the first beat back and forth under the needle. Get used to the strength of the turntable's motor as you scratch over the beat.
4 Then release the record just before the first beat by relaxing your fingers as you move the record forwards. As you do this you should give the record a minute push or flick with your fingers which allows it to move at the same speed as the platter. Remember to do this just before the first beat.

Keep practising this, making sure the track plays at the correct speed and place right away. It should become easy after half an hour or so. Soon it will be second nature.

CD DJs can slip-cue instantly using a button on the CD deck. See page 48, 'CD mixing'.

Beat mixing

Now we get to the exciting bit. Matching beats and then mixing them together is a key skill of DJing and it is not easy. There are no short cuts to mastering this skill. You simply have to practise. Once you have mastered beat mixing you will be able to blend two separate tracks of different speeds seamlessly together. Your audience on the dancefloor require this. Clang two records together – out of time with the beats mismatched – and watch the dancefloor crowd stop dancing and turn round and glare at you. You must be able to synchronise two tracks and to do this you need to practise. A lot.

The faders

Before you learn to beat mix though, you need to know how the faders on your mixer work.

The crossfader goes from left to right or right to left. It slides from one tune to another. Get a feel for this and you will notice that when the crossfader is in the middle the two tunes are of equal volume.

You can also fade in records by keeping the crossfader in the middle and using the upfaders. The upfaders (sometimes known as channel faders) adjust the volume levels for each particular channel. By keeping the crossfader in the middle, you can flip between tracks using the upfaders. Some DJs prefer using the upfaders but you can fade either way. It's good to practise both methods as the crossfader could be broken when you turn up for that all-important gig.

Some mixers let you change the speed at which the volume from the other channel comes in when you move the crossfader over. These are known as curve settings. A beat mix curve allows smooth mixing because the volume changes gradually from one channel to the other. Scratch DJs on the other hand prefer a scratch curve which lets the other channel in at full volume from only a small movement with the crossfader. This allows the crossfader to be used as an on/off switch – ideal for scratching.

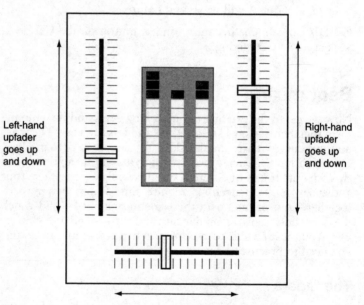

Left-hand upfader goes up and down

Right-hand upfader goes up and down

Crossfader can be moved from left to right

figure 13 basic mixer with crossfader and upfaders

Beat matching: getting the beats in synch

Referring to your left-hand deck as Deck 1 and the right-hand one as Deck 2, make Deck 1 'live' (i.e. Deck 1 is playing to the room). Do not touch Deck 1 as it is live. Any changes to this deck will be audible to the listener. All the work to create the mix will be done to Deck 2 through your headphones. This way only you can hear the adjustments needed to do the mix.

You should be listening to the beat of Deck 1 (i.e. the kick drum), getting a clear sense of it in your head. In other words you need to be very aware of the beat of the record playing to the room. This is after all the beat you will be matching the record on Deck 2 to.

At this stage the crossfader on the mixer will be all the way over to the left so that only Deck 1 is being heard. This ensures that no one but you can hear Deck 2. Now push the cue button for Deck 2. This will bring the sound of Deck 2 into your headphones. Now adjust the 'cans' (earpieces) of your headphones so that they are only covering one ear. This allows you to hear Deck 2 whilst listening to Deck 1.

Next find the first beat of Deck 2. Now you are ready to slip-cue. Push the first beat of Deck 2 back and forth under the needle in time with the beat from Deck 2. Then push it off so that it is up to speed straight away and matches the beat of Deck 1.

You now need to learn to synchronise the speeds. The key to this is to listen very carefully to both tracks at the same time that you push off. By concentrating you will be able to tell if Deck 2 is too slow or too fast. The more you practise this, the easier it will become.

With your right hand you are going to need to minutely adjust Deck 2's pitch control. How much you slide the pitch control is determined by how quickly the beats of the two tracks drift apart. First though, you need to bring the record playing on Deck 2 back into line by pushing it on (pushing the label around a little) or by slowing it down a fraction (using your left-hand fingers to apply a tiny bit of pressure to the platter or nipping the spindle between your finger and thumb).

Once the two beats are brought back in line you can then alter the pitch accordingly. If you had to push Deck 2's record on, it was obviously playing slower then Deck 1. The pitch (or speed) therefore needs to be increased. Likewise if you had to slow Deck 2's record, it was playing faster than Deck 1 and the pitch therefore needs to be decreased.

Watch any DJ beat mix and you will see them constantly tinkering with the pitch control. Pushing it up a fraction, then down a fraction. You need to get used to this as you need to be making adjustments to the pitch, whilst keeping the two beats in line. By listening to each adjustment of the pitch you will be able to get the two records to the same speed. By keeping them in line, using the tiny touches to the record and platter you have learned, you will also be keeping the two records in time.

Practice

1 Play Deck 1 live.
2 Listen to Deck 2 by using Deck 2's cue button.
3 Find the first beat of the record on Deck 2.
4 Push off Deck 2 at full speed in line with Deck 1.
5 Keep the beat of Deck 2 in line with Deck 1 by speeding up or slowing down the record on Deck 2.
6 Adjust the pitch control on Deck 2 to give it more or less speed so that Deck 2 synchronises to Deck 1.
7 If the records drift out of synch, make minute changes to the pitch whilst constantly listening to whether the two beats are now playing at the same speed.

Getting to this stage takes time and practise. Sometimes you will struggle to keep the beats in line and to adjust the pitch to the same speed. Sometimes the record on Deck 1 may run out before you have got it to the same speed. Don't worry – but do persevere. It will get easier and the more you practise the quicker you will be.

You will experience problems with beat mixing if your decks' motors are weak or belt-driven. This makes the platter move erratically, making it harder to keep the beats in line. Similarly, decks with badly-built pitch controls will make any speed adjustments difficult. Sticking to high-quality decks will make beat mixing easier.

Also beware of records that have live drumming in them. The tempo on these is likely to fluctuate. Be prepared to deal with this by making constant adjustments.

It is also worth noting that Technics 1200/1210s have two design faults. Firstly (as mentioned in 'Vinyl manipulation' earlier) it is easy to switch off the power switch by catching it on your sleeve. So keep your sleeves rolled up or wear a t-shirt. Secondly, and more importantly for beat matching, the pitch control has a minor but noticeable glitch when at 0. The pitch can waver around this point which can be annoying. You can slowly edge the tempo up or down on both decks and so avoid mixing around the 0 mark. Newer models of Technics avoid this problem, but some clubs may well have the older versions with the glitch. Remember this as it could throw you if you have learned on the newer, glitch-free models.

Blending

Once you can keep two records in time, you are ready to mix the two records together live. In other words you can keep the records in time so now you need to blend them together to create a seamless mix.

This is relatively easy. Simply beat match the two records and fade from Deck 1 to Deck 2 by moving the crossfader across. The upfaders should be up when you do this. It's best to crossfade slowly if you want a smooth blend so that the live sound goes gradually from one record into the other.

You can also do this by using the upfaders. Simply keep the crossfader in the middle. With Deck 1 live, the upfader for Deck 1 will be up, whilst the upfader for Deck 2 will be down. Gradually bring Deck 1's upfader down whilst simultaneously bring Deck 2's upfader up.

Whenever blending you should be constantly listening to both sets of beats making sure they don't drift apart. This will pretty much always happen so tiny re-adjustments are regularly required.

Drop mixing/cutting

Blending is great for house and techno where seamless mixes sound best. However it is useful to know how to drop mix, especially when you are playing pop, disco or funk. Drop mixing allows you to bring in a new record quickly without missing a beat. Hip-hop and R'n'B DJs will often mix using a combination of beat and drop mixing.

Drop mixing is essentially slip-cueing except you also move the crossfader to bring the new record in. Practise dropping the first beat of a track until you consistently start the record at the correct speed and on beat and then quickly bring it in. You might also drop it in at the start of a particular phrase rather than the first beat of the record. This allows you to jump swiftly from one record to the next whilst maintaining momentum on the dancefloor.

Practising this using two copies of the same record can help as it makes it easier to tell how accurate you are.

Drop mixing is also referred to as cutting because you cut between two records. You can cut back and forth between two records to create a juxaposition of rival beats which works well on the dancefloor, teasing the crowd. Cut from the end of one bar on Deck 1 to the beginning of a bar on Deck 2 and back to Deck I again at the end of the bar and so forth. This sounds more complicated than it is. It's actually a lot of fun.

The perfect blend

Having practised the art of beat matching, blending and drop mixing – whilst continually checking that your sound levels are correct – you should have a good grasp of the essence of mixing.

Now you need to fine tune these skills and learn some insider knowledge and tricks that will take your mixing to a professional level. Studying and practising this section will enable you to do well-thought out and smoother mixes. Audiences will love you for this. Your neighbours probably won't though.

Watching the sound levels

Before any mix is attempted it is essential that you make sure the sound levels match. There is no point perfectly beat matching two records if one is significantly louder than the other. If the record coming in on Deck 2 is too quiet, the audience won't notice the mix and will still be concentrating on Deck 1, so you will lose the dynamic impact of the mix. If the record on Deck 2 is too loud, blending into it will startle the crowd as it will be deafening compared to the record they have just been dancing to.

To make sure the sound levels match for each record, use the cue button to switch between each channel or deck. Look at the VU meter and see if the levels are the same. Many mixers allow you to do this at a glance by showing the master output and the cue output next to each other.

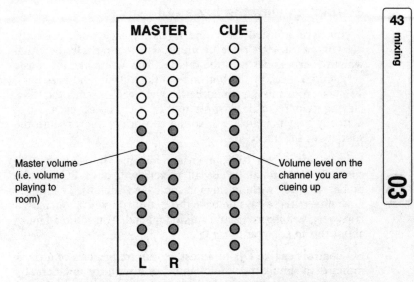

Master volume (i.e. volume playing to room)

Volume level on the channel you are cueing up

In this illustration the volume on the cue levels is louder than the master volume. This tells the DJ to turn the channel they are cueing down so that the track to be mixed in is not too loud.

figure 14 master/cue displays

This allows you to see which record is louder. You can then adjust the difference on the upfaders bringing the two sound levels in to line. You could also use the gain control or 'trim' if the mixer has them. These let you discreetly turn the volume up in small fractions for each deck or channel.

This is particularly useful if you want to play a track from an LP or a 12" that has more than one track on one side. The more tracks on a record, the quieter each track will be. This means you need to compensate by increasing the sound level (i.e. volume) for the channel that the track is on.

Failing to match the sound levels when mixing on a loud club system will sound terrible. You need to monitor and adjust them with each new mix. It's also a very good idea to make sure you leave some room on the sound levels by not having them at full. This gives you space to turn up quieter records.

EQ/Mixing with the bass out

If you have adjusted the sound levels for each track correctly, the volume of each piece of music will theoretically be equal when the crossfader is in the middle. This will make the music very loud, especially the bottom end (kick drum and bass line). To make your mixing sound better you need to remember this. Having two records play on top of each other, even when perfectly beat matched, can sound too heavy and obscure the subtlety of the music.

It is therefore best to compensate for this by using the EQ controls. Unfortunately not all mixers will have EQs, so be prepared to mix without them in some bars or clubs. Thankfully most mixers these days do have these controls which, when used creatively, will improve your mixing no end. You can read more about this in Chapter 04: 'EQ'.

EQ controls enable DJs to adjust certain frequencies of a track rather than simply the whole output of it with the upfaders. By concentrating on altering the bottom end (kick drum and bass) you can make mixes far smoother because you can maintain constant levels for these frequencies which are the loud part of any track. In other words be aware of the bottom end and use the EQ to adjust its volume and you will avoid loud and heavy-sounding mixes.

Practice

1 Turn the bass EQ control of Deck 2 down before you start to mix the record on Deck 2 in. (If you imagine the dial face of the EQ control is a clock, with its middle setting pointing up at 12 o'clock, you would be turning it down to about 8 or 9 o'clock.)

2 Keep the bass EQ on Deck 1 at 12 o'clock.

3 Fade in Deck 2.

4 As you do the fade, turn the bass from Deck 2 to 12 o'clock whilst bringing the bass on Deck 1 down. In other words swap the bass lines.

5 When doing this watch that the treble levels aren't too high. If so, take a little treble off from one of the tunes.

6 Be careful not to take the bass off Deck 1 until you have brought in the bass from Deck 2 otherwise there will be a noticeable drop in the levels.

Perfecting mixing by taking the bass out will make your DJing sound more fluent. You can also vary how you take the bass out by doing it gradually for more organic, long mixes or by quickly swapping the bass lines over. Let the type of tunes you play dictate how you do this. Experiment with it. It's fun.

Matching phrases

Unfortunately matching the beats and sound levels of two different tunes are not the only things you need to synchronise. It's also important to get the structures of the two tracks working together.

As we have already seen bars are regularly grouped together into 'phrases'. These are the building blocks of the structure of each track. A phrase is usually four bars long. Music is often arranged into four- or eight-bar phrases. New things happen in the music after phrases and it is useful to be able to predict this and use it to your advantage. The structure of a track might thus be:

- 16-bar intro
- 32-bar breakdown
- 8-bar solo
- 32-bar breakdown
- 16-bar outro.

DJs who perfect the skill of mixing will line up tunes' phrases as well as their beats. For example, a DJ would mix a 16-bar intro of the next record into the 16-bar outro of the record playing live. By doing this the phrases and therefore bars would all match and the mix would sound 'natural'.

Consequently you must be able to spot phrases. Listen carefully to a dance tune and spot where new elements are introduced or new drama is added to the track. These places will often be where new phrases begin. In fact there will usually be a musical marker at the end of each phrase such as a cymbal crash. Alternatively, you could simply count the bars, noticing how after every four bars there is a musical marker and another after every eight.

Dancers are instinctively aware of these musical patterns. Interrupting them (i.e. not matching the phrases) will interrupt their dancing so you need to get this right. It's not hard though – just remember to mix in a new record on the first beat of a start of a new phrase into the beginning of a new phrase of the record that is live.

Practice

1 Learn to be aware of the structure of your tunes. Spot new phrases by counting the bars of a dance tune. Notice the musical markers every four and eight bars. These markers could be cymbal crashes or extra drum beats.
2 Cue up the incoming record on Deck 2 so that it will play from the first beat at the start of a new phrase.
3 Mix it into the start of a phrase from the outgoing record on Deck 1.
4 Use the four- and eight-bar phrases as a guide for executing other adjustments/moves in your mix, e.g. swapping the bass in a blend; moving the fader another step in a blend; finishing fading out an outgoing record.

Once you perfect this the beats and events of your tracks will be synchronised. Your mixes will seem natural to your appreciative audience.

Mixing in key

Keys are groups of musical notes that work well together. Musicians play notes from the same key together because it sounds harmonious. Tunes and chords are made up of these groups of 'friendly' notes. Mixing notes from outside that key will often sound wrong or 'off key'.

This can be a problem because two tunes you may love might sound great separately but could sound dreadful together because their keys clash.

This can be avoided by using the split-cue button on your mixer to listen to the two records together before you mix them. Listen to the most melodic or vocal parts together and see if you can hear an out-of-tune sound or the two records still sounding out of time despite the beats being matched.

If you think there is a key clash between the two tunes it is probably best not to mix them and choose something else instead. Alternatively, cut between the two tunes without blending (see page 41, 'Drop mixing/cutting') or mix them during percussion parts when there are no vocals or melody.

It's also worth being aware that some dance records change key to add drama. Keep an ear on this.

Different blends

Use different styles of blending with the crossfader to vary your mixes and make your set more interesting. Mess around at home with two records that you know work well together and vary how you use the crossfader.

Practice

1 Slowly fade one piece of music into the other for gradual mixes. This works well with repetitive tracks.
2 Slowly fade in Deck 2, then smash the crossfader over. This can be good when mixing in a tune with a long drum intro before a vocal breakdown. You can mix the drums in slowly and then whack over to the vocal breakdown for high impact.
3 Overlay two records on top of each other. This won't work for all tunes but experiment to see which ones do fit snugly together. Long mixes like this will require your constant attention though in order to keep the tracks in time.
4 Quick fades are good for hip-hop tracks and music with live drumming. Rather than a long, drawn-out blend, quickly blend from one to the other.

Know your records

It might sound obvious but knowing your tunes well really helps. Some people will find this easier than others, especially people who are musicians. Good DJs will have mental maps of most of their records. They will know how long the intro is, where the bass line comes in, where the vocals start, where the breakdowns are and where the best part of the track to mix out of is.

By looking for these places and remembering them, you will have a great advantage when it comes to playing out to a real audience. Knowing your tunes this well will give you more time to do excellent mixes.

However, not everyone has the capacity for memorising thousands of tunes, but there are a few tricks that will help you do this. Record new tunes onto your CD or your MP3 player and listen to them when you are out and about. Keep listening carefully to the track structure. When you are packing your box for a gig, play or skip through the tunes you are taking to remind yourself of them. Similarly, when at a gig you can use the cue button to skip through the tune you want to bring in to familiarise yourself with it.

Doing these things will help make sure you know what is about to happen in any tune. This helps you know when to do mixes or tricks.

CD mixing

The same principles of mixing with vinyl apply to CD mixing. CD DJs therefore need to study the same art of beat matching and blending as vinyl DJs (see 'Beat mixing'). The only difference is that the machines and controls used to do this are different. Similarly, any vinyl DJ who wants to learn how to mix using CD decks needs to apply the same skills he or she already has whilst learning to use new buttons to execute these skills with.

CD DJs who wish to learn to play with vinyl will need to pick up the physical 'hands on' ability that vinyl requires, whilst vinyl DJs will need to get to grips with a number of new controls they won't be familiar with if switching to CD. Essentially though the key skills of concentrating and listening carefully to multiple sources of music are the same.

The truth about the two different formats is there are advantages and disadvantages with each format. For example, you can't instantly put the needle right where you want it in a CD track or put your hand on it to manipulate it, but on the other hand most CD decks enable you to create loops which you can't achieve on turntables. That's why it is best to learn to DJ with multiple formats. Not only can you play more music, you can perform more tricks.

Cueing up and beat matching with CDs

Cueing up your tunes on a CD deck is the main difference to vinyl mixing because you can't find your cue point by dropping the needle on the record. The cue point is the place you want to start the track playing, i.e. the first beat of a new phrase usually near the beginning of a track.

Search for the track you want by using the 'skip' or 'track search' button. You can flick through the numbers of each track on the CD by looking at the display. Most CD decks will have an automatic and manual cueing mode. Automatic is not good for beat mixing as it takes you to the first sound right at the beginning of the track. This sound won't always be the first beat so automatic mode is not good for beat mixing.

Cueing up manually is done using either a jog wheel (a rotary controller), a joy stick or search buttons, depending on which model you are using. These allow you to find the exact point just before the first beat. You can move to the nearest frame next to the beat. There are 75 frames per second which allows you to move very slowly, frame by frame, with great accuracy. You can then set this point next to the first beat as a cue point usually by using the cue button. This makes drop mixing easy as you simply hit play on the beat as you move the crossfader over.

Many CD decks now have a record-shaped interface which allows DJs to control the CD as if it were a record. This is great for scratching but also allows you to cue manually using the 'platter-like' jog wheel.

Once you have mastered setting cue points, beat matching with CDs follows the same principles as with vinyl using pitch control.

Practice

1 Play a tune live on Deck 1.
2 Find the track you want to mix in on Deck 2 using the skip or search buttons.
3 Scan through the track you want, using your headphones to listen, by using the search button, jog wheel or joystick. You can see where you are in the track by looking at the track counter on the display. Find the place in the track where you want to be.
4 Use 'pause' to pause the track.
5 Now use the jog wheel, search buttons or joystick to move very slowly, frame by frame, to the exact cue point just in front of the beat. You need to do this precisely so that you will start right on the beat.
6 At the precise place press 'cue' to mark your cue point. This is where the tune on Deck 2 will play from when you press 'play'.
7 Double-check the cue point by pressing 'cue'. Make sure it is exactly where you want it.
8 Now move your headphones so only one ear is covered. This enables you to listen to the live track on Deck 1 as well as the track on Deck 2 you have cued.
9 Press 'play' on Deck 2 in time to the beat of Deck 1. This should be in sync but if it isn't use the jog wheel or pitch bend to line up the beats exactly.

10 Decide which track is playing faster and adjust the pitch control to bring the tempos in line by speeding up or slowing down Deck 2.

11 Keep checking to see if the beats are now matched by hitting 'cue' to go back to your cue point and pressing 'play' in time with Deck 1. If they are not yet matched make further adjustments with the pitch control and keep checking back until they are.

12 When matched bring the tune on Deck 2 in on beat and at the start of a phrase.

13 You can make minor adjustments when the mix is live by lightly touching the jog wheel to fractionally slow the track or by pushing it on to speed it up, or if you have pitch bend controls you can use the two buttons to do the same.

With CD mixing you need to know the machine well. The controls on different models will vary. What's more, the sensitivity of crucial controls such as 'play' or 'start' or pitch bend buttons will vary hugely. Be aware of this. Practise on your own model but be prepared for the model in a certain club to be different. Right now the Pioneer CDJ–1000s are becoming the industry standard which makes practising easier. But these machines are expensive and there are other formidable models on the market which could be the ones you are faced with.

Looping

CD decks allow you to do digital tricks such as looping. This is great for extending sections of tracks or for making drum patterns to mix over or for making repeat vocal loops.

You need to mark the start of your loop by hitting the 'loop in' button at the beginning of the section you want. Then hit 'loop out' at the end of the section. Use the loop controls to fine tune your loop. Drop it in and play it until you hit 'exit' to go back to the rest of the song.

Master tempo

This is very useful for beat mixing because it allows you to change the tempo of a track without altering the pitch. In other words you can speed up a song without the notes bending. No more over-excited mouse choruses when you make those tiny tempo adjustments.

Hot cue

Some models allow you to lay down a cue point when the track is playing so that you can jump back to that exact part. On some decks you can lay down multiple cue points. This makes your own live edits of tracks possible. This is great fun but takes practice. Memory cards are able to store these cue points so you have them every time you play that track.

Instant reverse

This gives you the ability to spontaneously flip a track into reverse. It's fun but not that useful because who wants to listen to music backwards?

Digital mixing

Most people are now well aware of what an MP3 file is. It is a digital (i.e. non-physical) format for music – the same format that your personal mobile MP3 player, such as an iPod or iRiver, uses. Essentially they are compressed digital files of audio data. There are other formats such as WMA, WAV, AIFF, MOD, AAC, FLAC and MP4, but MP3 is the most widespread format. Mixing MP3s, or these other types of files, has become know as digital mixing.

From the DJ's point of view, the ability to use and mix digital music files is another exciting development. As with all technology it brings advantages and disadvantages – you would be foolish to ignore it though. Due to the audio file sizes, which are far smaller than the ones stored on CDs, it offers DJs the opportunity to carry their entire music collections on a single laptop. No more record or CD shelves. Tracks can be found instantly by searching your library of tunes. No more tearing your hair out as you stack pile upon pile of 12"s or CDs, trying to find that all important Daft Punk song. Added to this is the fact that the software available for mixing the files makes beat matching much easier as well as giving you all the pre-saved cue points you need. What's more, these files can be transferred through the internet which means that tunes can be sourced very quickly and often for free.

This all sounds magical to DJs and it is. It is rapidly changing the way we play. But there is a downside too. MP3 mixing software is still fairly fiddly. Computers can crash mid-set. But worse still MP3 files aren't great for sound quality. This is because some of the frequencies are lost when the music is compressed. You can notice the loss of these frequencies on a club sound system, especially the sub bass. If you are going to use MP3s it is a good idea to counteract this sound quality problem by compensating with the bass EQ control or better still using audio files with higher bit rates which are measured in 'kbps'. Most of the files you find on the internet are 128kbps. It is worth finding higher quality files at 192kbps or 256kbps. Some legal download stores offer DJs excellent quality files at 320kbps. These will obviously take longer to download though. Even these though won't sound as good as vinyl or CDs (but you would have to have well-trained ears to tell the difference).

Beware of file-sharing websites if you are a DJ too. The digital files on offer at these sites are, more often than not, of low sound quality. These are put up there by amateurs who don't have a DJ's requirements in mind. The file sizes will undoubtedly be too small for DJ use and will therefore sound poor on a large sound system.

A DJ who can mix using vinyl, CDs and MP3s has the world and its entire music at their feet. Technology should be embraced and mastered. Just remember to know its limitations too.

It is also important to realise the value of music both culturally and legally. Whizzing around the internet grabbing music might seem clever and easy but is it respectful? Making music is a musician's job. They need to get paid for it to live. Taking a music file without the copyright holder's permission is stealing. It is unlikely you'd be comfortable walking into a butcher, baker or candlestickmaker's shop and helping yourself to their goods and walking out without paying.

The internet has given people the opportunity to plunder the work of musicians and the recording industry that sells their music without paying for it. The music industry needs to be able to sell music if it is going to nurture and develop artists. If you love music be respectful of that. Illegally swapping or burning music files could even open you up to prosecution. Increasingly, lawsuits are being issued against people who obtain music illegally. The best advice is to use legal download services such as iTunes, TuneTribe, DJ Download, Bleep.com, Karmadownload or ClickGroove. Note that these download stores will use different file types and sizes.

It is also worth being respectful of the cultural significance and history of the artists you love. There are no sleeve notes informing you about the music you are about to listen to on digital files. It's worth making the effort to learn about who made the music you like, how they did it and why it might be important culturally. This will give you more music knowledge and, chances are, make you a better DJ.

The choice for digital DJs

Aside from burning digital music files on to audio CD–Rs and mixing them using CD decks, there are two ways of DJing with them. You can mix them on a computer using special mixing software. Alternatively, you can use mixing software on a laptop alongside specially-designed hardware. This is often preferable for working DJs as it combines the advantages of digital technology with more 'hands on' control.

MP3 mixing hardware can come in the form of a dual CD-style console which allows you to cue up and play MP3 files just as you would a CD, or, as in the case of Stanton's Final Scratch, specially designed turntables and vinyl.

You will still need to use a mixer to mix the tunes if you are using a console or vinyl emulating hardware.

Mixing MP3s on a computer

Using a powerful laptop you can mix MP3s using your mouse and keyboard with software that creates virtual DJ mix stations. You can choose from as many tracks as you have stored and browse easily just as you would find a document on a computer.

Software packages such as AtomixMP3, MixVibes or MP3DJ give you full cueing and pitch control for beat matching. Some will even beat match for you making a DJ's life easier still. Don't for one second think this means you can instantly become a great DJ. It definitely makes mixing easier but you will still require all the other skills a DJ needs such as programming (see Chapter 05: 'Programming and sets').

The best packages to use for professional mixing on screen are probably the Native Instruments' Traktor DJ series which enables laptop mixing with MP3 and other files. Traktor DJ Mixer allows you to see tracks playing in graphic waveform. This means you can clearly visualise upcoming sections of tracks. Matching phrases is therefore easy. It has EQ, kill switches, beat counters and automatic beat alignment which takes the pain out of matching beats. It even has filters and pre-set scratches. Traktor DJ Mixer can only be used on PCs though.

The improved Traktor DJ Studio 2.6 is designed for live mixing, remixing and mix recording with MP3, WAV, AIFF and audio CDs, and can be used with Macs as well as PCs. It is also compatible with Final Scratch 2.0. The price is around £130.

Using such software does make mixing very easy. It also enables you to create loops or edit your tracks, creating your own unique versions which you can do live or pre-recorded.

Mixing MP3s on consoles

Using a mixer, computer and software you can mix MP3s on CD-style decks. Numark's DMC-1 consoles are perfectly adequate. Native Instruments have also developed a piece of hardware which has a double-deck panel to run alongside Traktor – the Hercules DJ Console. This costs in the region of £170.

As with CD decks one of the disadvantages is that you can't move a needle to different parts of a track, you need to search through it, but you can of course save multiple cue points. As with laptop mixing software this technology also allows you to continually edit tracks and create loops.

Mixing MP3s on vinyl emulating hardware

There are now quite a few purpose-built units for mixing digital files, often with the ability to swap to CDs too. You could use CD deck-like equipment such as the Technics SL-DZ1200. This is the first direct-drive digital turntable. It looks, and more importantly, feels like spinning vinyl on the Technics 1200 turntable. The slip surface of the 10" platter allows you to spin, scratch and manipulate tracks in a number of formats including CD, MP3 and AAC. You can store, play back, scratch and loop files from a removable memory card. It's clever stuff and gives you real flexibility with different music formats.

Deck-like machines, purpose-built for DJs who want to use digital files, therefore work to a large extent like contemporary CD decks. The music still needs to be beat matched, phrases still need to be adhered to and mixing is still done using mixing units (mixers). In other words you still need to learn the principles of mixing set out in the bulk of this chapter.

Stanton's Final Scratch system on the other hand allows you to mix digital formats of music in the analogue way. Using a powerful laptop that stores your music files, an interface unit connects these to a normal pair of turntables and a mixer. Using two specially designed 12" pieces of vinyl you can effectively create virtual decks that can be used just like their analogue cousins but with all the benefits of digital technology.

This is very attractive to DJs who have developed their skills using vinyl. They can store thousands of tunes on a single laptop and manipulate them by hand as if each was a record. Any of your music files can be 'transferred' to one of the special pieces of vinyl and scratched, rotated, cued and used to mix as usual. The interface does this by working out how fast and in what direction the special vinyl is moving in.

This method also allows you to mix MP3 files with good old-fashioned vinyl. You could have a normal record playing on one deck, and an MP3 file playing on the specially made vinyl on the other deck.

Mixing on Final Scratch is therefore the same as mixing vinyl. You still need to know your tracks well so that you can match phrases and appropriate styles. You need to beat match using the decks' pitch controls as is normal with vinyl DJing. Likewise, mixing the tracks together is done using a conventional mixer with the upfaders or crossfader.

To summarise, digital mixing makes DJing easier largely because of the ability to store massive amounts of music digitally but also because it enables the creative DJ to chop up and re-organise tracks. Using CD deck-style units or the Final Scratch system allows you to DJ with digital files much like you would with vinyl. Using digital mixing software on your laptop even allows you to 'cheat' at mixing by helping you beat match.

Yet despite all this you still need to learn core DJ skills such as blending or programming. You also need to beware of the inferior sound quality of some digital music files. Make sure you sound good. It is a good idea to record your vinyl into digital format yourself, or if ripping your CDs, do it yourself to the best possible kbps for MP3 or convert them to WAV or AIFF files. Don't rely on an inferior quality file an amateur has created and put on to a file-sharing website. These are likely to be of low quality and will sound poor on a club sound system. Make sure you control the sound quality of your music, and make sure it is good.

DJs who learn to incorporate digital technology into their sets will have an advantage in the competitive world of DJing. Because programmes like Ableton Live enable you to remix tracks live and blend music that has erratic beats, your sets will be far more creative and original than other, more traditional DJs. By embracing this technology you can make a name for yourself through your unique, mind-blowing, sensational sets. You might just be the most exciting DJ in town.

04 tricks of the trade

In this chapter you will learn:
- what DJs do to make their mixing perfect
- how to wow an audience with insider tricks
- how to discover the art of scratching.

Even your long-suffering neighbours are probably fairly impressed with your mixing skills by now. With regular practise you will have mastered the art of moving skilfully from one tune to the next. As we have seen, this is done in a seamless blend so that your audience is not interrupted from the raptures of their dance moves, or in a cutting style that jumps from one beat to the next with the crowd's blessing.

You now need to learn how to mess with their minds. This is where the rule book is less important and you get creative. Of course DJs want to keep people dancing but they also want to wow them, tease them and trick them. To do this you need to learn the small tricks and toys that DJs love to throw into the mix.

EQ

The EQ on your mixer is there to help improve your sound. With the EQ controls you can adjust different frequencies, usually 'treble', 'mid-range' and 'bass', although some mixers may have two mid-range controls for the bottom and the top of the mid-range. You do this to manage a tune by, for instance, taking the treble down a little if a vocal section is sounding a little screechy, or if you want to soften a hi-hat that is too loud. Or you could turn the bass EQ up a bit if the kick drum or bass line on a track is slightly weak.

As we have seen, DJs also use the bass control to blend and swap bass lines when beat mixing (see Chapter 03: 'EQ/Mixing with the bass out').

So DJs use the EQ controls to give the audience a smooth ride, this much we know. However, DJs will use anything at their disposal in their unending quest to make the dancefloor bounce like a trampoline. They like to be able to seamlessly mix from one track to another but they also like to use the equipment at their disposal to make people go crazy. The EQ controls are good for this.

Most good mixers will allow you to adjust the treble, mid and bass for each channel. This means you can add drama and contrast to a track. For instance, you can take the bass out four bars before a build-up in the music. Your audience will be aware of this and will be dying for the bass to come back in, which you drop back in right on the big build-up. This will send them wild.

You can also do this using 'kill' switches. Some mixers have 'kill' switches or buttons which turn off a complete section of frequencies, i.e. 'kill' or cut out the treble, mid or bass. These are fun and useful but not essential if you have other EQ controls.

Using the EQs you can also highlight certain parts of a track, encouraging further audience response. For example, you could turn the mid up a little during a particularly mad, spacey noise. This will exaggerate the noise and thus send your dancers into orbit. Be careful to do this in moderation. Too much mid-range can sound terrible.

You can also use the EQs to mix between different elements of two tracks, i.e. place the kick drum and bass of one track under the vocal of another. Be careful that you don't do this too much. It's easy to get it wrong.

It's also easy to mess around with the EQ too much. Use it sparingly. It can sound a bit overbearing.

Practice

1 Take out and slam in the bass. Cut the bass completely by quickly turning the bass EQ to 0 or by pressing the bass kill switch. Do this just before the first beat of a bar and then bang it back in on the beat just as something dramatic happens. Knowing the track's phrases will help.

2 Exaggerate the treble when taking the bass out causes the dancefloor to squirm as the effect is not pleasant. Turn the treble back to normal as you slam in the bass and the crowd will respond with yelps of pleasure because of the tension, and then release, you have created.

3 Cut the mid and treble for a dark, horror sound of booming bass. Then flick the mid and treble back in on a vocal breakdown and soak up the whoops of joy. Again, there is no gain without pain.

4 Highlight certain instruments or noises to add drama. Turn up the mid during a siren sound to extenuate it. Or during a particularly long bass line and percussion section where not much happens you could bring up the mid to highlight the congas or bongos which the crowd should respond to by getting all tribal.

5 Drop the bass in and out during a long drum section to maintain the crowd's interest.

6 Try using different elements from different tracks together. Try the bass line from one under the vocal or melody of another.

Bear in mind that some mixers may not have EQ controls on them or will simply have EQ controls for the overall sound rather than for each channel. Boring but true.

FX

Advances in digital technology continue to blur the boundary between the DJ booth and recording studio. Although dub reggae DJs have used effects like echo for years, effects that were out of the reach of DJs are now available to add yet more drama and UFO-type noises to your set.

Effects units (or FX boxes) process the signal from your mixer and mess it up into desirable contortions. These regurgitated sounds can be used much like the EQ controls to add drama and tension to your music. It is best to experiment at home with them before you use them live at a gig. Get a feel for how they interact and enhance the music.

Again though, effects should be used in moderation. Too much will overshadow the essence of what makes your music good in the first place. It is far better to use them on stripped down pieces of music rather than heavily produced songs that are already stuffed with clever sounds.

Also remember that to use an FX unit during a live mix, you will have to be pretty dextrous as your hands will need to fly from mixer to FX unit to CD deck/turntable and back again.

Which units?

Some mixers and some CD decks have built-in effects. Whilst it is fun using them, the effects could well be covering for the poor, overall sound quality of the machine. It is always best to buy a mixer with superior sound quality than one with effects if you are on a budget. If you can afford it the Pioneer DJM-500 is great to use, with good sound and a myriad of effects for under £400. The Pioneer DJM–600 is even better at around £600. Bear in mind that to do the same effects at a gig, you will need to bring the mixer with you.

figure 15 the Pioneer DJM-500 mixer with built-in FX
source: Pioneer GB Ltd

Stand-alone FX boxes are easier to transport. They simply connect to the club's mixer and are operated through the 'send' button for each channel on the mixer.

Many of these units can be gimmicky and sound great in the shop before you actually use them in a live situation. The original Korg Kaoss Pad was not very DJ-friendly as it was hard to accurately repeat the killer sounds it could create due to its touch sensitive screen. The Korg Kaoss Pad KP2 is an improvement at around £200. It has numerous new effects operated by an easier-to-use interface.

The Gemini DSP-1 DJ effects unit (around £140) has over 1200 sound settings that can be made to fit the tempo of your music automatically. The Pioneer's EFX-500 (under £400) allows you to isolate its numerous effects to different frequencies so that, for instance, they only affect the bottom range. Its more expensive brother, the Pioneer EFX-1000, is pricey at around £699 but a great piece of kit with 24bit/96kHz digital sampling giving very good sound fidelity.

figure 16 the Korg Kaoss Pad KP2
source: Korg

Overall, you need to be able to access the FX quickly without having to set any times such as the length of a delay. Therefore you need a box that reads the tempo and has easily accessible controls. The ability to make loops is also a nice bonus. Be careful not to buy a box that adds unwanted hiss to the mix – cheap ones may do this. Also be aware that some FX boxes favour different genres with built-in sounds added in to suit that genre be it hip-hop, techno or trance.

Common FX

Effect	What it does
Delay	Makes timed echoes of a sound to add depth.
Distortion	Adds a dirty, grungy sound just like you get when you turn up your amp too loud.
Echo	Beloved of reggae sound systems, echo repeats the sound whilst fading away.
Filtering	Filters out certain parts of the sound.
Flanging	Adds a whooshing sound by mixing a delayed version of the sound with the original.

Gating	Cuts the track up to produce a rhythmic, staccato effect.
Phasing	Gives music a wavy, flanging effect.
Reverb	Adds the ambience of a space, i.e. makes an audio signal 3D. Sounds great on voices and drums.

Classic tricks

It is surprising how a few well-placed tricks or mixing embellishments can add excitement to a set. An audience will always respond well to a set that is made that bit more dynamic by being punctuated with some showy gestures that give the music further impact. It's always a good idea to have a few tricks up your sleeve even if you are only wearing a t-shirt. Here are some classic moves.

A cappella mixing

Mixing an a cappella vocal (the vocal part of a track separated from any musical accompaniment) over the beat of another record can be very effective in giving a well-known song new context. You could try playing an a cappella version of an old disco or pop track over a modern house beat or an a cappella version of a well-known rap over completely new beats to create your own bootleg.

Be sure to choose the tracks you mix your a cappella over carefully. The vocal needs to fit the groove and sit harmoniously. If the vocal is out of tune with the other track it will sound awful. Make sure you experiment with what works well at home before you try it live. Get it right and the dancefloor will love it.

Practice

1 Choose an instrumental that fits your vocal well.
2 Listen to the original of the vocal to find which beat of the bar the vocal starts on. A cappellas rarely start on the first beat of the bar so generally you need to listen to the original to get the timing right. Count as you listen so you can work out on which beat to drop mix the a cappella in.

3 You will probably need to change the speed of the a cappella during the mix. To do this use the pitch control rather than manipulate the record or jog wheel otherwise the dancefloor is likely to hear changes in pitch to the vocal. Use the pitch control during quiet moments in the vocal.

4 There is more room for error when mixing a cappellas because there are no beats to clash, but this also makes it difficult to get the tempos right as there are no beats with which to judge each track. It's best to listen to the groove of the vocal by paying attention to how the vocalist begins and ends the words for each phrase. This will help you keep the mix in time.

Line-in/phono switch tricks

The line-in/phono control on a mixer is actually there to switch between which signals a channel receives, i.e. you are meant to use it to flick between a channel receiving music from a turntable or CD deck for instance. DJs have learnt to use the line-in/phono switch in another way. To do this you need to make sure your turntable or CD deck is the only device plugged into a channel so that the line input on the back of the mixer is empty.

Now you can toggle between the music playing on that channel and silence. Why would you want to play silence? Because it adds contrast to the music. Switching from music to silence is dramatic if done well. You can cut up a capella vocals taking out lines of the song or rap. Or you can isolate the kick drums in the mix by flicking out everything except the 4/4 beat. Alternatively you can make a long drum passage more interesting by chopping out a new rhythm on it.

Practice

1 Make sure your turntable (or CD deck if you are a CD DJ) is the only machine plugged into a channel on your mixer so that the line input is empty.

2 Flick the line-in/phono switch on and off and you will hear the music be cut up with silence.

3 Learn to do this in time with the music, e.g. flip to silence on the off-beat and back to music on the beat to emphasis the kick drum. This takes a bit of getting used to as your natural tendency will be to do it on the beat.

4 Experiment cutting whole lines or, if you are quick, words out of raps or songs again by flicking the line-in/phono switch on and off.
5 To do this quickly it is best to practise using your thumb and forefinger to tap out rhythms with the switch.

Sometimes when a mixer is pretty battered and old as many of them are in clubs, you may get a crackling sound when you flip the line-in/phono switch. For this reason, and simply because you may prefer it, it is a good idea to learn to how to do these effects using the faders. They are just as effective but you will need to practise doing them quickly as it obviously takes longer to slide from one end of a fader to the other than it does to flip a switch. Make sure you have nothing playing on the opposite deck when trying these moves.

Fills

Another common and similar move is to cut from a track playing to a snippet of another and then back again. Breakbeat, drum'n'bass, UK garage and grime DJs tend to do this a lot. The basic move here is to cut to the record you are about to mix in for the last bar of a phrase and then flip back to the original. It's a good way to tease the crowd with what you are about to play. In other words fills are good for introducing new tracks. This can obviously be done the other way too so that you keep cutting back to snatches of the track you just mixed out of. Once you have perfected this try creating new beat patterns by bringing in beats from another tune into the bar. To do this you will need good coordination and a well-defined sense of rhythm.

Practice

1 Make the track on Deck 1 live.
2 Cue up Deck 2 and make sure the sound levels match.
3 Whack the crossfader over to Deck 2 for the last bar of a phrase and then swap back to Deck 1.
4 Practise swapping bars throughout the phrase. Form a pattern that fits in with the phrasing.
5 Try bringing in beats from Deck 2 into the bars of Deck 1 to build new rhythmic patterns. This is great for breakbeats.

Spinbacks

We've all heard people shout 'rewind!' during a popular tune. Rewinds are particularly common practice in drum'n'bass, hip-hop and reggae DJing. If your audience demands a rewind you will need to be able to do a spinback. They are pretty easy to pull off if you get the timing right and they sound really startling because it reminds the audience you were in the mix.

A spinback is performed by suddenly putting a record into reverse. You can do this with the reverse button on a CD deck, but it won't sound as good as on a turntable because the CD deck will reverse the tune at a constant speed whilst a turntable will run out of momentum when spun back giving the spinback great-sounding definition. Some newer models of turntables have reverse buttons, but it still generally sounds better when done by hand.

Practice

1 With Deck 1 live, on the last beat of the last bar of a phrase, spin the record on Deck 1 back sharply on the slipmat. Then very quickly cue back to the beginning of the track to play the 'rewind' of the same tune.
2 If you want to go from a rewind into another record, with Deck 1 live, on the last beat of the last bar of a phrase you want to mix out of, spin the record on Deck 1 back sharply on the slipmat. Crossfade over to Deck 2 on the first beat of the next bar so the timing goes 1, 2, 3, spin – new tune.
3 Alternatively, for a more blended effect, mix the tune on Deck 2 into the end of the tune on Deck 1 and perform the spinback just as something dramatic happens in the tune of Deck 2, such as a bass line coming in or a breakdown, and fade across to Deck 2 on full volume.

Be careful when performing spinbacks to make sure the needle doesn't fly off the record. This can happen if the record is warped or if the hole for the spindle is too tight. Make the hole a little bigger if necessary.

Power downs

This is easy and sounds dramatic but can be a bit annoying if done too regularly. A power down is simply done by turning off the power to a turntable that is playing. It causes the platter to slowly grind to a halt and therefore the music slows and loses momentum before coming to a complete stop.

This is best used for dramatic effect to introduce a new, really dynamic tune.

Practice

1 With Deck 1 live, turn the power off on Deck 1 at an appropriate place in the tune. Don't press 'stop' as this would be too sudden. Actually turn the power off.
2 Pause for effect.
3 Then whack on the beginning of the new powerful tune. Make sure it does not have a long, drawn-out drum section at the beginning which will be sure to lose audience interest. A mad spoken word intro could be good here to raise the drama, e.g. some American dude with a deep voice talking about how the power of the music is going to save all mankind.
4 Alternatively, don't pause for effect after the power down comes to a halt, instead go straight into a punchy piece of music on the beat.

You can also use power downs to end a set at the end of the night.

Of course you can also use the stop button on decks for more instant stops. You need to be pretty confident to do this as if you don't go into the next track quickly enough and it doesn't sound right, you are likely to have a lot of bad vibes coming your way from the dancefloor.

Phasing

By playing two copies of the same record and creating a tiny delay between the two you can make a song sound like it is whooshing.

Practice

1 Beat match two copies of the same record in exactly the same place in the track.
2 Make sure they are playing at equal volume and have equal EQ levels.
3 With the crossfader in the middle, slow the pitch of Deck 2 slightly to get a whooshing effect.
4 Before the two records go out of sync, move the pitch of Deck 2 so it goes slightly faster. The same effect will occur as the record on Deck 2 catches up to Deck 1.

5 If the whooshing effect isn't happening, listen to see if you can hear two kick drums. If you can, the delay between the two needs to be smaller so make a tiny manual adjustment.

Back-to-back mixing

Again this involves two copies of the same record, but this is less subtle than phasing and more likely to be picked up by the crowd. Essentially you play the same track half a beat apart whilst cutting in extra beats from the second copy of the same tune.

Practice

1 With only Deck 1 live, beat match two copies of the same record in exactly the same place in the track.
2 Make sure they are playing at equal volume and have equal EQ levels with only Deck 1 still live.
3 Now on your headphones, slow the pitch of Deck 2 until it is exactly half a beat behind Deck 1. You will hear double the amount of beats per bar at double tempo.
4 Now fill in bars of Deck 1 with extra kick drums from Deck 2 with swift moves of the crossfader. Make sure you always return the crossfader to the next kick drum of Deck 1 so that the 1, 2, 3, 4 time of the dancefloor is not lost.

As an alternative you could play two copies of the same record back-to-back with Deck 2 half a bar behind Deck 1, by cueing it half a bar behind and then cutting between the two. This can be dramatic if not overused.

Mixing on three decks

This isn't advisable unless you are a very accomplished beat mixer. For a start you will need to practise it at home which means forking out for another deck (or borrowing a friend's). It's not impossible as it obviously follows the same methods of beat matching, but it is fiddly because it requires constant three-way monitoring. It can be effective for mixing a different mix of the same track together with the original and one other. It's also an effective way to put an a cappella, spoken word or sound effects over two other tracks. But ultimately it is a bit of a waste of time and only that impressive to people with too much time on their hands.

Beat juggling/looping

With the in-built sampling technology found on many mixers and CD decks today, only dedicated turntablists still practise the manual art of beat juggling or looping. The roots of beat juggling lie in the 'looping' technique that DJ Kool Herc developed in the early '70s. Speed is all-important and it works well with scratching techniques (see 'Scratching').

Practice

1 Use two copies of the same record, preferably instrumental hip-hop.
2 Find an easy section at the front of the record. You could mark the beginning of the section with an arrow on the label or a small piece of tape on the record. Hip-hop DJs do this so they can place the needle straight onto the required beats. It will be best to start practising by using a four-bar section to give you time for rewinding.
3 Cue both records to the front of the section you want to play.
4 Play Deck 1 live to the room.
5 As soon as the four bars have finished, drop mix the first beat of the record on Deck 2, crossfading straight into it.
6 Immediately rewind the record on Deck 1 to the first beat of the section.
7 Drop mix Deck 1 in at the end of the four bars of Deck 2.
8 Keep switching between the two until you get faster and faster.
9 Start practising this with a two-bar section, then a one-bar section, then half a bar, etc.

If you can do this at high speed without missing a beat, you are ready to start incorporating some scratching techniques.

Some musicians and DJs argue that it is disrespectful to the original producer of a track to have DJs chopping it up. The truth is DJs have always messed with the music at their disposal – it is all part of being a creative DJ.

Having learned all the tricks you can use to wow, impress and work a crowd, you now need to grasp the importance of not overusing these tricks. Crowds don't like being battered over the head by an endless assault of brain-numbing tricks. Instead use them to enhance the music. Your number-one job is to play the most appropriate music. In other words use tricks in moderation. Unless of course you are a scratch DJ …

Scratching

Scratch DJing, or turntablism as it is also known, is all about the art of scratching records and turntable tricks. Scratching was invented by Grand Wizard Theodore in New York in 1977 whilst he moved the same part of a record back and forth under the needle. From this was born a DJ culture of its own where decks are used as instruments to play bits of sounds from records which are cut up using the mixer.

Scratch DJing is a culture in which you can flex your skills and show off your moves until your heart is content. But be sure the skills and moves are good. Competition is fierce and your peers will take it very seriously.

To begin you need to learn the basics of scratching.

Preparing to scratch

You can pretty much use any record to scratch as long as it has got an assortment of beats and other sounds such as vocals. Old tracks with great breaks are obviously great here as these are where hip-hop has its origins, but you can use a normal 12" record. Alternatively, if you want lots of samples and beats on one record, go for one of the battle breaks compilations found in hip-hop shops.

You may need to enlarge the hole where the platter's spindle goes slightly so it can turn freely. You may also want to mark certain key parts of your records with small stickers so you know where your cue points are. Your slipmats need to be very slippery. It's best to use ones without printing as this causes friction, or better still, cut out two circle-shaped pieces of plastic inner sleeve from a record and place them under your mats.

Deck-wise Technics still lead the market for scratch DJs but Vestax models are also used because of their straight tone arm which helps stop the needle jumping.

You can help prevent the needle from jumping by applying extra downward pressure, but this will increase the wear on both your needle and vinyl. To do this, either have the counterweight on the tone arm set fully in, or turn it round and then set it fully in which supposedly gives the tone arm even more weight. Alternatively, you could increase the height of the tone arm if your turntable allows, altering the downward pressure on the needle yet further. It is not advisable to place extra weights on

Some scratch DJs like to keep the tone arms out of their way and therefore position the decks on their side in 'battle style' formation.

figure 17 decks and mixer in battle style formation

your cartridge such as small coins as this will seriously reduce the lifespan of your needle and records.

Set up your decks and mixer in the formation that is easiest for you. Most clubs will have the decks either side of the mixer in the position they were designed for with the tone arm on the right. Scratch DJs usually prefer to move them to a 'battle style' formation.

If you have the choice on your mixer set the crossfader to a scratch curve so that you can chop up scratches with less movement. If your mixer only has a beat mix curve, you can still use it, you will simply need to move the crossfader further to do the same moves.

Some mixers have what is known as a 'hamster switch' which allows you to reverse the left and right channels on your crossfader which in turn enables you to combine certain moves. These switches might be marked as 'X-fader assign'.

When you are scratch DJing, both your hands will be making rapid movements either on the fader or the record. It is a really good idea to try to practise all the moves you use with both hands so you can be more versatile.

The good news is you can hold the record wherever you like. It's about what feels right for you.

The baby scratch

If all this talking of scratching is making you itch, now you can try your first scratch move without using the fader.

The baby scratch is the classic 'wukka-wukka' sound and it is the basic starting point for all scratching. It involves moving a record back and forth under the stylus.

Practice

1 Pick a funky record and find a part in it with a long sound. Any percussion, voice, or synth sound will be good.
2 Hold the needle still in front of your chosen sound whilst the platter spins beneath.
3 Keeping your hand well away from the tone arm, move the record back and forth so that you make a 'wukka-wukka' sound under the needle.
4 Do this faster and slower to notice how it affects the tone of the scratch.
5 Improve your control by doing one scratch on the first beat of the bar, then one on every beat of the bar. This should build the intensity of the scratch.

You can now start messing with the sample of sound you are playing by dividing it up and playing different parts at different speeds. Try playing the sample forwards as normal, then pull it backwards, but this time stop it dead quickly before finishing the back stroke slowly. This way you can cut the scratch up and change the sound of it.

Forward scratch

Now you need to learn to use your mixer to define your scratches. This works as if your turntable were a sampler taking snippets of sound. You use the mixer to release certain parts of those sounds. You can use the upfader to take out the back stroke of a scratch so that you only hear the forward stroke. This is forward scratching.

Practice

1 Hold the record with one hand and the upfader with the other. The upfader should be down so you can't hear the record.
2 Perform a forwards and backwards scratch under the needle.
3 As you do this open the fader on the forward stroke and then close it on the back stroke so you only hear the forward stroke. Both your hands should be moving almost in unison as you do this. In reality there is a minute delay between each of the four movements: fader up; play sample forwards; fader down; rewind sample backwards.
4 Your fingertips should stay in the same place on the vinyl so that you don't lose your spot when rewinding the sample.
5 You need to be able to drop samples cleanly and at speed, so keep practising until you get faster.
6 Play forward scratches together in rhythmic formation to form a beat.

Back scratch

Changing the previous manoeuvre slightly you can perform a back scratch by cutting out the forward stroke and playing the back stroke.

Practice

1 Pull the fader down.
2 Play the sample forwards (you won't be able to hear it).
3 Push the fader up.
4 Rewind the sample. This time you'll hear it.
5 Again practise this at speed and in rhythmic formation.

Rub/stab

By keeping your hand on the record when you push it forwards you can experiment speeding up or slowing down the sample. When you slow down and decelerate the sample by hand when it's playing either forwards or backwards, it is called a 'rub'. When you keep your hand on the record and push it forward live you will be giving the sample a high-pitched effect. This changes when you do it backwards. This speeding up of the sample is known as a 'stab'.

Scratching to the beat

It is a good idea to practise your scratch moves to music. Put a beat-heavy, low tempo track on one deck, and practise doing your scratches to the beat.

Transforming

Transforming is the art of using the fader to cut up a long scratch into a series of rhythmic bursts.

Practice

1 Find a long sound to use as the sample.
2 Perform a slow backwards then forwards scratch. Let some of the sample play normally for a short while.
3 Starting with the fader closed, rapidly open and close it to chop up the scratch into a rhythm of your own.
4 Practise this at different speeds with different sounds.
5 You can also use the line-in/phono switches to chop up the scratch. Or if you have transform buttons near your crossfader, you can tap these to cut the other channel in quickly.

You can perform a reverse transform known as a 'flare'. To do a flare start the scratch with the fader open and use it to turn off the scratch.

Fades

You can scratch with an echo effect by bringing the upfader down a little more with each forward scratch. This sounds good with vocal samples.

Chirp

Bird-like chirping sounds can be created fading out of a forward scratch and then performing a back scratch whilst fading back in.

Scribble

A series of short, very fast scratches performed by the hand making a quick shivering movement.

Beat juggling/looping

Developed by DJ Kool Herc, this technique of flirting between the beats of two records at high speed is often incorporated into scratch DJing (see page 62, 'Classic tricks').

In this chapter we have covered the fundamentals of scratching but this is by no means all there is to learn about it. You have learned only the basic moves. There are numerous other techniques, each with their own variations. Being able to learn and perform these techniques is one thing. It's another to be able execute them as accurately as possible during a live performance whilst maintaining a dazzling sense of rhythm. An audience needs to feel a constant sense of tempo whilst gawping at your myriad of impressive skills. This is, after all, DJ showmanship at its most creative.

Now go and develop what you have learned into your own style. Watch battle videos and read everything you can on the subject to learn from those who have developed the different techniques (see Chapter 12: 'Taking it further'). There are no rules but to strive to be as inventive, as accurate and as funky as possible.

05

programming and sets

In this chapter you will learn:
- how to pack your record box for a gig
- how to play at different times of the night and at different type of events
- how to get the best possible reaction from the dancefloor.

So now you can beat mix, blend, cut, do tricks such as spinbacks and even scratch. You have mastered the art of DJing, right? Wrong. You have mastered the mechanics and moves of DJing. You know how to use the equipment and how to work different tracks together. But the next stage of learning is about taking a step back from the mixing and looking at how the music interacts with your audience and also the venue. The art of DJing is as much about picking the right music for the right moment as it is about mixing. What's more, you need to know how to programme music over the length of a set, how to start, develop and end a set and indeed how to play at different times of the night. The structure of your set is crucial to this. Do it right and you are far more likely to get a great reaction from those dancing.

Researching and preparing for gigs

Playing in a club to a paying audience is a very different experience from playing at home to yourself. There are two major differences:

Firstly, DJing on a large sound system is a world away from your home hi-fi. Records sound very different. In fact they sound much larger. Much of the subtle and deep parts of the music get lost on a booming sound system. The crashing percussion and thundering bass dominate the room. This can be a real shock for first-timers. Don't worry about this too much, because at the same time, many records will sound great as they have been specifically made to be played on loud club sound systems. Others, though, may sound weak in comparison. A thin kick drum or bass line will be shown up to be weak.

The second main difference between DJing to yourself and your cat, and a large crowd is the fact that whereas your cat may grin and bear what you play, a crowd won't. In other words, for the first time, you have to think about what other people want to hear, rather than what *you* want to hear. The tracks you love and sound great at home may be completely inappropriate for other people. It's no good taking a load of tunes that don't make people dance when you get a booking. It is therefore essential that you research where you are going to be playing and prepare for your set. That way you are far more likely to give the crowd exactly what it wants. This is what you are being paid for after all.

Research the gig

If you have played at the same venue before you will have a good idea of what to expect. If you haven't you must try to find out as much as you can about where you are due to play. You need to know what time you are on, who you are playing before or after, what genres work on the dancefloor and preferably what sort of set up they have in the DJ booth.

The best way to find out such information is to go to the venue a week before, when the same promoter is running the night, and check it out for yourself. Take a look at the booth and type of mixer you will be using. Watch the dancefloor and see which types of record get the best reaction. If it's a house night, is it tech house or deep house or funky house or vocal house that gets the punters jumping up and down? If it's a hip-hop night, does early rap get the best reaction or cutting-edge independent hip-hop or is it the DJ's turntable skills that they are most interested in? Soak up the atmosphere, think about what you might play and how you could do even better.

It's also a good idea to chat to the promoter and get their view on what the crowd loves. Ask other DJs you know who have played at the venue about how it went and what to expect. Bear in mind though, other people's perception of what makes a night work could be miles away from your own. Many DJs have fallen into the trap of relying on other people to tell them what to bring. It's always best to make your own judgement.

If you can't get to the venue yourself make sure you know whether the night is a gay, straight or mixed one. Is the audience largely female or male? Is it a young crowd of fun seekers or a place frequented by Northern Soul fans. Any information like this helps you make an informed choice as to what music the crowd might go for.

Prepare for the gig

Now that you have a better idea of who you will be playing to, you need to think seriously about what music you are going to take. Taking the wrong music can be disastrous. You don't want to be looking sheepish next to your box of roots reggae 7″s whilst an R'n'B crowd sits down around the edge of the empty dancefloor. You need to choose the music you take carefully.

Find a selection that reflects your style as a DJ, but also caters to the crowd you will be playing to. Don't grab any old pile. Instead, find the tunes you think will make that particular crowd dance like possessed rabbits. Don't think you have to play what everyone else is playing, i.e. all the current big anthems. It's not a bad idea to take a couple of these dancefloor bombs, but it's important to make sure your set is individual too. The world is full of DJs playing the same music. It doesn't need any more. Don't copy others. Be yourself.

Being individual could mean mixing up your record box with old and new tracks; fast and slow; forgotten gems and the odd classic; or prepare some unreleased productions from your friend in the studio. To put it another way, you obviously want the music to make the audience dance, but you also need the ability to surprise. As a DJ you need to entertain but you also need to be daring, and perhaps even educate a little. It's those standout tracks that you will be remembered for.

Don't feel you must be cutting-edge trendy either. Keeping your ears tuned into the lastest music is no bad thing, but playing brand new music for the sake of it is not much fun for others. It depends where you are playing, but as a rule it pays to drop in great, old material with new tracks. It makes for a good contrast and helps lead your dancers into new pastures as if you were holding their hand with the older records before exciting them with the hot new stuff.

In my experience, unless you know the club and crowd very well – for instance, if you have a residency there – it pays to take more rather than less music covering different styles, moods and tempos. This way you be well prepared to react to circumstances.

Make sure you don't overprepare for any one set though. A set you have fully worked out at home is unlikely to translate well to a live environment. Instead you need to pack your box carefully and be prepared to be flexible to the crowd's needs. I've made the mistake of playing the same set at two different venues in one night. The set went down so well in the first club, I thought I would do practically the same set again in the next club. The reaction was completely different the second time around. I had been lazy through tiredness and I paid the price with a lacklustre dancefloor. I learned never to take a crowd for granted.

Judge what each crowd wants and manipulate your set accordingly. This is where the key skill of reading a crowd comes in (see 'Reading the dancefloor').

Arriving at the gig

It's always worth getting to a gig a little early. This gives you the chance to soak up the atmosphere and hear what's being played. Crucially though, it also gives you time to adjust the sound system before you start your set.

Don't do this from the DJ booth as the sound in the booth is likely to be different from the dancefloor. The DJ booth may be enclosed and the acoustics will therefore be different. Go on to the dancefloor and have a good listen. Is the system sounding lifeless, dull, bass-heavy or too piercing with too much treble? Go back to the booth and re-adjust the bass, mid-range and treble on the EQ until the sound is full of life. However good your mixing is, your set will sound tired if the sound is poor.

As we know from Chapter 03: 'Mixing: The perfect blend' you need to be constantly watching the volume levels too. A sound system is much louder when a venue is empty. This is because the sound waves echo off flat surfaces such as walls, and because people's bodies break up sound waves thus lessening their impact. Remember to keep sufficient room on the master volume level on the mixer especially at the beginning of the night. This gives you the space to turn the volume up as the venue gets fuller. You don't want to be in a situation where the music is getting quieter as the club fills up and you can't compensate with the master volume. Anyway, no one wants to hear deafening music early on in an evening. As they arrive people will probably want to chat and have a drink by the bar.

Now you need to set the monitor volume level. You need good monitoring as there will always be a sound delay between different parts of a club. Set it so it is loud enough to hear the music's rhythms but not too loud so that it tires your ears. Standing all night next to a speaker at high volume will not help your mixing at all as your ears will suffer fatigue.

Once you have set the monitor levels, set your headphone volume. This should be marginally quieter than the booth monitor. This will make it easy to mix in the new tune without deafening yourself. You'll also be able to hear what's happening on the dancefloor whilst mixing if your headphone levels aren't too high.

Reading the dancefloor

Reading the dancefloor is yet another key skill of DJing. You must be able to judge what an audience requires. You need to be aware of how much they are enjoying themselves. You need to know when you should change the atmosphere by playing a new mood or style, or by taking the tempo up or down. Without this ability you might as well be a jukebox or someone who just plays mix CDs. You are there to interact with the audience. You are there to take them on a musical journey, the route of which you alter in response to the dancefloor.

In other words you need to be incredibly sensitive to the dancefloor and those around you. DJing isn't about giving the masses what you want. It's about giving people what they need and taking them somewhere else if the time is right. You guide rather than pull them along.

So how do you find out what all those people are thinking? It's not so easy but it is a skill that you will develop with experience. The essence of it is to soak up the atmosphere and watch the crowd.

Are they mainly female? If so, they may well prefer more songs and vocals. Are they a gay crowd? If so, which type of gay crowd? They may want something faster or more disco-influenced for instance. Is the dancefloor packed full of trainspotters? In which case you can take more risks and perhaps play more obscure electro or underground techno. Is the audience older or younger? An older crowd might prefer music from a different era. What are they wearing? If they are wearing a lot of black with cruxifixies around their necks perhaps you should be dropping some goth classics. Seriously though, what they are wearing is important. Is it a very fashion-conscious crowd who demand the latest imports from Cologne and Japan, or is it a relaxed crowd who needs a bit of guidance?

Other aspects of the crowd need to be considered too. Drugs and alcohol will affect how the crowd reacts. They change people's perception of the music. A drunken crowd is obviously likely to be more rowdy and the chances are they'd prefer to hear tunes they already know. They probably aren't in much of a state to struggle with new crazy rap tracks. A 'high' crowd, on the other hand, is likely to have loads of energy and be keen for you to play accordingly. Intoxicants make people react differently and you need to respond in the right way.

A dancefloor that is packed with a large crowd will be much more forgiving than one with a small crowd. A small crowd's tastes are much more noticeable as it will be obvious when they go and sit down during a track they don't like because the dancefloor will be empty! However, the taste and whims of a select few will be lost on a busy dancefloor. A large crowd will have more momentum and energy and will therefore be harder to play the wrong thing to.

Looking at a crowd gives you all sorts of clues. Watching their reaction to music gives you even more insight to what makes them tick. If a Hoover bass line sent them potty earlier, drum'n'bass could be the way forward. If they responded well to slower tunes, you could gradually bring the tempo down. Be observant to their reactions and respond accordingly. This way you should win their trust.

You can even be a little experimental with what you play once you have won the audience over. You can try different moods and styles and see how they go down. Don't be tempted to play crowd pleasers all night as this is likely to be overbearing. You need to guide them through your set rather than whack them over the head with anthems.

Programming

Putting tunes in the right order is more important than mixing: fact. What's the point of perfectly mixing a hands-in-the-air anthem at 10 p.m. into a really deep instrumental dub? There is no point, because, however good the mix was, you will have played the wrong music at the wrong time. You need to learn the art of programming.

Programming is an art. Unfortunately you cannot pick it up by practising at home. It is something you instinctively pick up over the years. Essentially it is about knowing exactly the right tune to play next.

It is a terrific feeling when you have a full dancefloor of people really enjoying themselves and you know exactly what to play next. In fact, sometimes you vibe off the situation so well that you know what the next three or four tracks are going to be.

Key to knowing what to play next is a concise grasp of how each of your tunes works on the dancefloor, i.e. the feeling and energy it creates. Different tunes have a different impact on the dancefloor. It helps to recognise this and remember how a track stimulated the dancers last time you played it. In other words, did it make them start spinning on their heads, did it get them punching the air in delight or did it slow the dancefloor down?

If you are perceptive you can work out how much energy different tunes give the dancefloor. You can probably already guess which records will work best for a warm-up or peak-time set. You need to develop this instinct further by constantly monitoring dancers' reactions and developing a mental database of how your music affects people.

How energetic records are is crucial, but so is their style, mood, tempo and even rhythm. Although a record can be in the same genre it might have a different style or flavour. For instance, a house record could be dubby, jazzy, soulful or rocky. A drum'n'bass tune could be deep and melodic or dirty and heavy. You can therefore influence the dancefloor by shifting the energy, mood or style of the music.

You can also choose music by its tempo or rhythm. Again, it's important to build a mental library of which records complement each other by their tempo or rhythm. You might want to heat up the dancefloor by introducing more percussive rhythms full of bongos in order to get those hips shaking.

You can, of course, also pick the next tune because you know that it works well with the previous one from experience, or you think it will work well because you remember that it has a similar bouncy bass line or similar Latin-flavoured rhythms.

Good DJs will always be thinking ahead to the next couple of records. It can be really helpful to pull any tunes you think might work out of the box and sit them diagonally on the top so that they are flagged up and you can see which ones to choose from.

To summarise, by being perceptive enough to judge what the dancefloor needs through people's reactions, you will get a feel for what to play next. That decision about which new bit of music to play is influenced by the colossal mental map of your own music developed by getting to know your tunes well and seeing how they work in a live environment. You can then select new tunes according to their energy levels, their pace, their mood, their style or rhythm. You can therefore pick a record that is perfect for the moment. You will then know that the record you pick to cue up will work with the tune playing and that it is right for the dancefloor.

By pulling records out of
the box and sitting them
diagonally in the top, a
DJ can find the records
they want quickly.

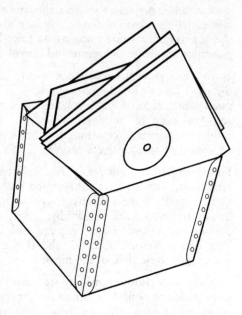

figure 18 record box with record sleeves sitting diagonally

By choosing the right record for that moment you will be
making sure you maintain the dancers' interest and keep the
momentum of the dancefloor going. Yet, and this is where the
fun part comes in, a set is never a static thing. An experienced
DJ will also be programming for the future as well as the
moment. He or she will be choosing music that works for the
dancefloor but also progresses the set, i.e. the set is a journey
with different sections. A clever DJ will usually know exactly
where he/she wants to take a crowd. In fact he/she might have
two or three tunes that he/she knows they want to play towards
the end, in order to finish on a massive high. The set could be
built with this in mind. Always trying to progress the dancefloor
to a level where it is ready to have those particular killer tunes
dropped. The DJ is therefore leading the crowd as well as
responding to them.

Sets aren't static then. They are steered by the dancefloor and by
the DJ's desire to take the music in a specific direction. If you are
playing before another DJ, you should also consider what they
are likely to be playing.

If a set is a musical journey, it needs some sort of pace and structure. There are different ways of doing this for different occasions. First, though, you need to know how to shape a set.

Shaping a set

Why bother giving a set a structure? Why not just play crowd pleaser after crowd pleaser? Well, the answer is, you could. But you would be overindulging the audience. It would be like going out to a classy restaurant and instead of enjoying a slow, three-course meal, going straight for the chocolate cake dessert. It would taste fantastic, but leave you feeling strangely unsatisfied, if not a little queasy.

Remember that people who have paid to get into a club are probably going to be there for a good few hours. Give them back-to-back screamers for too long, too early and they are going to be tired out too quickly. You need to think about your set in the context of the whole night. This is where pacing comes in.

The type of set you play depends largely on what time of night you are going to be playing. If you are playing first, before the venue has time to fill up, you can afford be more eclectic and to play slower, gently building an atmosphere as the dancefloor fills up. Alternatively if you are playing at a peak time such as 1 a.m., your set structure will be different and the pace will be more energetic.

Your set should therefore fit with the time you are playing, but it should also fit the amount of time you will be playing for. Unfortunately most DJ sets these days are limited to two hours. This is great for cramming as many gigs into one night as possible but not great for really taking a crowd on a long musical journey with the chance to play many different styles.

Your set should have a beginning, middle and end just like a good story. You use the beginning to set up what you are about: it's an introduction bringing a crowd into your style of music. The middle is where you can create peaks and troughs, taking the atmosphere and energy levels up and down, giving the dancers a chance to draw breath after each peak. The end is usually where you build towards a high impact finish, perhaps a classic or new version of a well-known track.

However, this formula wouldn't work for a warm-up set or an end-of-the-night set. These must be specifically tailored for the energy levels on the dancefloor. Again, an all-night set would be more of a collection of different musical sections. Gentler styles might give way to more energetic dance music. Then you perhaps would move into an eclectic selection, before ending on an hour of classics. DJs such as François Kevorkian, Laurent Garnier and Danny Tenaglia are masters of this style of all-night sets.

Whatever the length of the set, it needs a beginning, middle and end. These sections can be punctuated with tricks or musical changes. Likewise the element of surprise should be used to keep people literally on their toes.

This all helps to create drama which a good set definitely needs. We've all been to nights where you can hardly remember any of the music played the next day. This is likely to be because the DJ kept his set on one level without ups and downs and no sense of drama. Music should be exciting unless of course you are a chill-out DJ! But even then it should be thoroughly stimulating.

Keep these criteria in the back of your mind when shaping your set

1 Structure

The structure of your set depends on when and how long you are playing. If you only have an hour or two you will probably want to build towards a peak, gradually increasing the energy levels until everyone including the bar staff are dancing on the tables.

Given more time it is satisfying to learn how to introduce different styles of music, showing a crowd how one style is perhaps connected to another. Start off slowly and then build things up, before taking the audience back down, and then back up again. Ups and downs in the energy and the music gives the dancers time to recoup before the next moment of madness.

However long you are playing, you should use your knowledge of your music to use the various moods, tempos, rhythms and energy levels in your record box to shape the set to best suit the night. Pace your set right and you are far more likely to have a full floor.

2 Building tension/release

Rather than giving an audience hit after hit, or underground track after track, you should be aiming to create drama. As we have seen, varying the mood and tempo helps do this by making sure the set isn't predictable and flat.

Another great way to make your set dramatic is to build tension and then give release. The trick to this is to gently increase the energy levels with each new record whilst hinting at the climax to come. This could be done using repetitive but hypnotic tracks which you mix together before a big pay-off tune.

Alternatively, you could do this by playing snippets of a well-known song. Keep doing this for a number of tracks without playing more than a small section such as a couple of bars. Then after teasing the crowd, whack in the whole song and the place goes potty.

Another way is to build tension and release within a single track by using the EQ to take away certain elements of the music, such as the bass, before bringing it back in for maximum impact (see Chapter 04: 'Tricks of the trade: EQ').

3 Punctuation

DJs will often punctuate their sets to help give them definition and maintain the dancers' interest. This could take the form of a sudden change in style or tempo; or a complete stop in the music or a wind down. This gives the dancefloor a chance to pause for breath before some more great music. The key to pulling it off successfully is to have won the trust of the dancefloor. You wouldn't try this halfway through a warm-up set. The floor needs to have been responsive to you for a while before you can try it; they need to know you are pausing on purpose. Do it right and it will add to the excitement because they will trust you enough to know that you are going to come back with something phat.

4 Surprises

Be brave enough to use the element of surprise. Pick the right kind of surprise for the right moment and the audience will love you for it. This is what will make you stand out from other DJs. It could even become your calling card – but maybe then it wouldn't be much of a surprise!

So how do you astound a crowd? Catching them unaware with an old classic is one more obvious way. You could catch them off guard by dropping a completely radical change in genre such as a cool, funky rock track in the middle of a dance set. You could play the original track that a well-known sample comes from having just played the version that uses the sample. This works well in hip-hop sets. You could stop the music and play something with a dramatic spoken word intro before the music comes thundering back in. Or you could give them a bolt from the blue by playing a secret weapon of your own, such as an obscure psychedelic funk record, or a tune they have never heard in a club setting such as the theme to 'Knightrider', which as it happens is rather good.

Leave your crowd open mouthed by using an element of surprise in your set.

Different styles of sets

Sets come in many shapes and forms. Here's a look at some of the main differences.

The warm-up

Warming up is likely to be the first type of set you get bookings for. There's a real skill to warming up well. Unfortunately it is a skill many inexperienced DJs ignore. New DJs are often to keen to play their anthems, loud and fast. That's fine at the appropriate time of night, but it will sound dreadful in a warm-up set. There is simply nothing worse than pounding dance music on an empty dancefloor.

A warm-up set is all about laying the foundations of the night. It's your job to hold back if warming up. Look to build the atmosphere gradually rather than deafening people as they arrive in a club. Most people want to relax with a drink when they arrive. The music needs to reflect this mood. The dancing will come later.

That's not to say you should be playing boring music. Far from it; your music should be very engaging. This is your chance to play those weird records you have been wanting to hear; to play things out of the ordinary; to play slower tracks and perhaps some older music. This is an opportunity to play more than one style. As a music lover, you should welcome this. Make sure the music is interesting and inspired and you will engage the audience as it starts to grow. Soon people won't be able to hold back and they will begin to float on to the dancefloor, pulled in by the magic of your tantalising music. By intriguing people and gradually building the atmosphere, you will be leading dancers to the dancefloor in a very natural way. Remember to build the tempo slowly without rushing.

Girls will often start dancing before boys, perhaps because they are less self-conscious. Try to target them in order to start getting the dancefloor going. Playing tunes with vocals may well get them on their feet.

Once you can tell that people are itching to start dancing – because they are hovering around the edge of the dancefloor and there is tangible excitement in the air – it's a good idea to give them a killer tune that you know will push them over the edge and on to the dancefloor. This is the tipping point; the instant the club comes to life. This is a moment of great joy for DJs. Now the fun can really begin.

Peak-time

A peak-time set needs to deliver everything a crowd on the dancefloor wants and more. Your aim is to maintain the momentum of the dancefloor whilst taking the dancers for an exhilarating ride.

Your set could build tension by increasing the energy levels bit by bit or it could have ups and downs. However you structure a peak-time set, you need to keep the dancers locked to the floor and wow them with your dynamic mixes and perfect track selection.

If you are nervous hold your resolve. Play tunes you know well and enjoy yourself. This is what all the hard work has been about.

End of the night

The end of a night has a different mood from the rest of the evening. There may only be a few dancers left or people may be tiring out a little, or the place could, and hopefully is, still packed.

You could respond by giving the dancefloor small rests by playing less energetic music here and there. This can be dangerous though as you don't want to lose the floor entirely. Instead it's best to be inspired by the crowd. You should have by now watched the audience close enough to really know what sets them off. Now's your chance to give them styles they love. You could hold their interest by playing quirky tracks or give them some surprises. You could play some unexpected genres to shake them awake. Old or forgotten classics may well work well at this time of night too. You might well want to end on a high, or perhaps with a song with positive meaning. That way people should go home with smiles on their faces.

All-night set

The first thing to remember if playing all night is to bring more music, of course. You are going to need far more than the average two-hour set requires. Bring different styles and different genres and old gems from the depths of your collection.

A long all-night set should be thought of as a long story, once again with a beginning, middle and end. It might even have other chapters in between. It should be made up of different moods, tempos and styles. You will, after all, be playing the warm-up set as well as the peak-time set and the end-of-night set. You need to be able to master all these different types of set skilfully and put them together into a coherent and dynamic whole.

Make sure your all-night set is well structured, builds tension and release, has punctuation and a lively amount of surprises. Without good structuring it is likely to be flat and even confusing to the dancefloor.

Make sure you have eaten before a mammoth set, watch your alcohol intake and use those lovely long records to nip to the loo.

Bar sets

DJing in a club is usually a very satisfying experience as everyone is there to hear your marvellous music. With bars though, people are there mainly to drink and look at members of the opposite sex. Music is more of a background device used to build the ambience. That's not to say people won't dance, but you shouldn't have your heart set on a set full of club anthems. Instead opt for a more mellow selection, perhaps use the opportunity to be more eclectic, dig out those tunes you have been dying to hear but have never had the chance to play. Remember, your job is to set a welcoming and lively mood for the bar, not to blow the speakers.

Wedding sets

Wedding sets are easily the most difficult types of set you may ever be asked to do. It's a misconception to think that all is required is a string of oldies that will have all the drunken revellers dancing. It is indeed about tunes that people know well, but it is no easy task to play music that appeals to all generations. You need to be able to get the grandparents on their feet, whilst making sure you play exactly what the bride and groom have requested, and at the same time keep the teenage nieces and cousins happy. Take oldies, take chart hits, take slow dances and expect to take many, many ridiculous requests.

DJing between bands

This is the easiest type of set to do. Everyone there, probably including yourself, is there to see the bands playing live and for precisely that reason are unlikely to give a damn what you play. It's your job to play music between the bands whilst people queue up for hours trying to buy warm lager in plastic glasses. It's not your job to give a DJ performance. Instead, perhaps concentrate on playing music that you think might have influenced the headline band. The audience should appreciate this. Do not in any circumstances play anything by the headline act; it will take expectation away from their performance. Oh, and make sure you are ready to drop that tune *after* the encore, not before.

Corporate events

These events are distinguished by two things. Firstly by the fact that you are being paid ridiculous amounts of money to play at this event. Having a DJ is a desperate bid on behalf of the company to look cool and they should be paying you way over the odds for your entertainment. And secondly, these events are distinguished by the fact that nobody is actually listening to the music. The structure of your set is therefore completely irrelevant and you might as well play what you want. Do smile and give a thumbs up sign to the CEO when he walks up to you to offer a vol au vent. Be warned however, selling your soul is a beautiful thing for your bank manager but a terrible thing for your passion.

Fashion shows

A DJ set at a fashion show is nothing like a club set. It's not your job to respond to the crowd. Instead, you will be asked to rehearse with the models and fit music that perfectly captures the feeling of the collection as they walk up and down to a set time. This is great work if you can get it. Your set needs to be tightly rehearsed and the timing should be immaculate. No peeking behind the curtain into the models' changing room though.

Radio shows

There is no dancefloor to worry about when you are on air. Tempo and energy levels are far less relevant. Instead, structure your show around cohesive styles and moods of music. Make sure everything you play is engaging to your audience and present it all with dynamism and clarity.

See Chapter 08: 'Turning pro: Playing on the radio' for more details.

House parties

Whatever anyone tells you – whilst playing to two thousand people on a sound system the size of Manhattan is indeed fun – the ultimate DJ experience is to be found in your average two-up, two-down home. A set at a house party is a rare treat. Why? A house party is likely to be full of your mates, meaning that you know the crowd well. No second-guessing what they might like, you already know this inside out. This makes it all the more fun. You can rip the roof off (don't do this if it's your own house though). What's more, you aren't playing to any music policy that a venue might have. Play what you want, just make sure people are dancing on every available piece of furniture and that the neighbours are banging on the door with the noise-pollution police. You might have to DJ next to a pile of mouldy washing up in a kitchen, but you should have an awful lot of fun. You can even play tunes with lines like: 'We're going to have a house party ...'

06

the dancefloor

In this chapter you will learn:

- how to deal with stage fright
- how to deal with things that can go wrong when you are playing live
- how to respect your ears and other DJs.

Dealing with nerves

It's completely natural to be a little nervous before a gig. Many veteran DJs still get butterflies when they are about to play, especially at a new venue where they may be unsure of the crowd's response or where they might be unfamiliar with the equipment.

Playing to a large amount of people is intimidating. It is a very different experience to playing at home. At home you have perfect monitoring; no one is trying to talk to you whilst you mix; and, of course, there is no one to make dance. In a club on, the other hand, tunes that sound great in your living room can sound weak on a large sound system. Also there may well be one or more people hassling you whilst you are trying to mix. And there will certainly be a lot of people who expect you to entertain them.

The pressure is on. But don't let it get to you. Believe it or not, whilst all DJs may be nervous to some extent, a very nervous DJ sounds nervous. Confidence is a crucial part of DJing. Without it, it is easy to let the equipment and music dominate you. A flustered DJ sounds flustered. A nervous DJ may lack the confidence to pull off really dazzling mixes and may well not trust his or her own instinct when it comes to choosing the next song.

There are a number of ways you can make sure you cope well with playing live to an audience. Following these guidelines can help ensure you have the confidence to perform to the best of your abilities so that you concentrate on the job in hand. There are a number of things you can do to make sure you remain confident and pin down those butterflies.

The essence of beating your nerves is knowing your job. That's why DJing gets easier the more experience you have. Knowledge is power after all. Follow this advice and you'll laugh in the face of fear.

Know your tunes

All DJs need to know their records well. This is easier said than done as you are sure to be getting through a lot of music. When you get sent or buy new music, sit down with it and let it soak in. Put it on to your personal MP3 player and listen to it whilst doing the shopping.

Practise mixing new tunes so you become familiar with them. Knowing your tunes inside out means you won't come across any nasty surprises. You'll know if a record is too quiet to be played out or if there is a particularly tedious breakdown in the middle of your new 12".

Knowing your music therefore helps you avoid mistakes but better still it also helps you mix like a disco devil. Intricate knowledge of where vocals begin and end, where breakdowns start and finish, where drum patterns change all mean that you know where best to blend, cut or scratch tracks together.

This knowledge will give you self-assurance. Knowing your tunes well will give you the confidence to perform well.

Research the gig

Knowledge is also power when it comes to playing at a new venue. Taking a booking for a place you haven't played before means you need to find out about where you will be performing and to who. Arriving at a new gig unprepared means you will be faced with equipment you haven't used before and a crowd you don't know.

Go online and find out as much as you can about the club night beforehand. Speak to other DJs you know who have played there and ask them what it was like. Ring the promoter and ask them what equipment you will be using. Ask them if they can install your favourite machines (some will oblige, many won't). More importantly, ask about the type of audience. Is it gay, straight or mixed? What music do they normally respond well to? Is it a cheesy night or strictly cutting-edge tunes? What time will you be playing? Who are you playing after?

Better still visit the club the week before and see for yourself what records are making people go mad. Have a look at the DJ booth too.

All this information will help you make an informed choice about the music you take and how you play it. Knowing the gig before you get there will give you more confidence and therefore help fight nerves.

For more ways of researching a gig see Chapter 05: 'Researching and preparing for gigs'.

Be prepared for the unexpected

Take music for any eventuality. Even a thoroughly well-researched gig can throw up surprises. You may have been booked to play hip-hop, but when you get to the venue the dancefloor is empty apart from a big birthday party full of friends who want to hear funk. You need to be able to deal with situations such as this as they do arise.

The best way to prepare for any eventuality is to take more than one style of music. Taking two boxes of records seems like a pain in the neck, not to mention back, but it could be a good idea if you are playing a new venue for the first time. Taking different genres or sub-genres of music gives you more ammunition in your quest to make people dance. See Chapter 05: 'Researching and preparing for gigs' for tips on packing your box.

However, do make sure you are using tunes you know well rather than drowning in a sea of vinyl that you are not familiar with.

Know how to deal with things when they go wrong

Technical problems cropping up during your set are guaranteed to make you more nervous. Yet by being aware of what can go wrong and knowing how to resolve these problems, you can spot difficulties quicker and respond to them.

See 'Dealing with disasters' later in this chapter.

Take deep breathes

By controlling your breathing you can reduce your feelings of panic. When people are nervous or have had a shock (such as a record running out!) your body produces adrenalin. Adrenalin is a natural hormone designed to help us deal with frights. It makes the heart pump faster which is useful if you are being chased by a tiger because it means you can run faster. Thankfully, however, there aren't many tigers in night clubs. But by getting nervous you will be producing adrenalin which will make you feel agitated. You can help suppress this feeling by taking big, deep, slow and steady breaths. Doing this for 30 seconds or so will reduce your heartrate and help make you feel calm.

Don't panic

Deep breathing will help you remain calm but so will a bit of good old-fashioned mind control. Think it through. You know you can mix well. You know you have some great tunes. You know these tunes inside out. You know you can do it.

Remind yourself that you have the ability to DJ well. It's all going to be all right. In fact you are going to wow them.

Get the crowd on your side

Start off with some tunes the audience knows. Once they are dancing and you are past your first few mixes, you'll begin to relax and vibe off the crowd. Win them over and you'll soon be putting yourself at ease.

Have fun

Enjoy yourself. You and they are there to have fun. That's what music is all about after all. If you do a bad mix, so what, it happens. Move on and get caught up in the atmosphere. Bringing great music to people is a beautiful thing.

Stage presence

As an entertainer you need to look the part as well as sound right. Luckily you don't have to dress in platform shoes and wear a suit made of silver glitter. You can wear what you want, but it's a good idea to look like you are enjoying yourself. An audience will pick up on the power of the music and your brilliant mixing, but they will also pick up vibes from your body language. Seeing a DJ really enjoy what they are doing is a great thing to witness and encourages the crowd to let themselves go more. Think about how much Fatboy Slim dances around and punches the air when he's DJing, or the positive vibes Norman Jay gives off when he's enjoying himself on the microphone at the Good Times Sound System at the Notting Hill Carnival. Their enthusiasm for the music is infectious. In other words it's not just the energy of the music that counts, but the energy you give off as a performer too.

Whether you are DJing at large club in Ibiza Town or a small bar in Nottingham, you are to all intents and purposes on stage. The DJ booth may be a table with decks on it in a corner; it may be a purpose-built booth towering above a massive dancefloor; or it could literally be on a raised stage. Whatever the set-up, you are there to entertain a crowd and you should be aware of your body language because the crowd will notice it.

Consequently don't hide behind the decks. Don't run onto the dancefloor and start hugging people, but do be proud of your music and enjoy the moment. Getting really into the music you are playing means you will do better mixes because you will be caught up in it like the dancefloor is. When they respond to a big tune or a great mix, look at them and beam from ear to ear. Let them know you are relishing it as much as they are.

With this in mind it's probably a good idea not to sit down whilst you DJ, or eat a meal, or read a book, or have a nap. I've actually seen DJs do all these things and more. None of them are likely to help the crowd jump up and down with hands in the air. The sight of one DJ in particular completely fast asleep whilst he was meant to be mixing is not something I'll forget in a hurry. Nor will the people who were there who couldn't believe their eyes or ears as the record ran out.

Furthermore, it's worth noting that large alcohol consumption pre- or mid-set isn't likely to make you a better mixer. A drink might well help calm nerves but five drinks could seriously impair your judgement. The ex-pat West Coast DJ, Harvey once compared drinking and DJing to driving. Drink and driving don't mix, nor does drink and mixing. Drink too much, and as with automobiles, you are likely to crash. People want a smashing set, not beats that are smashing.

Be proud of what you do. Don't be a glory-seeking twit wearing shades whilst playing air guitar to the crowd. But do have a good time. You are playing the music you love after all.

Dealing with requests

Whatever type of venue you are playing you will always get requests. Some will be inspired, some unacceptable, most just plain stupid. Even at a underground hip-hop night in the Bronx someone will probably ask you for some pop music. DJs love comparing the daftest requests they have received. It's almost a sport. From 'Have you got any funk music?' when you are playing James Brown, to 'Can you please play my favourite music?' when you have never met this person before.

Requests can be annoying especially during that all-important mix. I've even witnessed a DJ punch someone who kept requesting the same record again and again having been told that it wasn't going to get played.

Instead of getting upset about requests, see it as part of the job. It's a good idea and good manners to always react politely. Most people don't think twice about DJing. They may well not appreciate the skill or concentration that goes into it. They might therefore start hassling you even when you are busy. Nevertheless, deal with the situation professionally. If they have the guts to ask about a record they love give them your attention. They are after all helping you by letting you know what at least part of the dancefloor wants to hear. If the record fits with your set why not play it? If it doesn't or you simply don't have it with you, let them down gently by saying, 'Sorry but the tune is at home.'

Sometimes you might get someone who is verging on psychotic about the song they want you to play. If they are causing a problem firmly explain that you won't be playing it and that they have to leave the DJ booth or you will be forced to call security. This works fine unless it is security who is hassling you in which case smile and say, 'Why certainly, Sir.'

Top five worse requests (all true):

1 'Can you play some dance music?' – requested during Donna Summer's 'I Feel Love'.
2 'Can you keep the music down, I'm expecting a call? – requested at around 1 a.m. in Fabric, London.
3 'Can you play some hip-hop without rapping?'
4 'Can you sing Happy Birthday on the microphone? It's my boyfriend's birthday.'
5 'Can I have a go? I've always fancied myself as a bit of a DJ.'

The correct answer to these requests is of course, 'Please go away and never speak to me again' but instead the actual answer given in these situations, through gritted teeth, is: 'Umm, interesting idea. Maybe later' ('later' as in 'never' that is).

One DJ I know answered request no. 5 spectacularly by saying 'Yes, sure'. He walked away to the bar to get a drink and left the lady in question behind the decks. It goes without saying she was somewhat embarrassed when the music stopped and hundreds of people began shouting at her.

On a similar note it is a good thing to be helpful to punters who ask about the tune you just played. It shows appreciation of your music. Telling them about the artist helps switch people on to new exciting music. Being the music enthusiast you are, you've probably asked a thousand times yourself. So be polite and why not show them the record or even write down the name of it for them.

Dealing with disasters

What's the worse thing that can happen to a DJ? A clanging mix? A jumping needle? An ex-boyfriend/girlfriend walking up to you mid-set? No. The worse thing that can happen when you are entertaining a crowd of dancers is for the music to stop. It's that simple. It is every DJ's nightmare.

However much preparation you do things can and will go wrong in a live environment. Speakers can blow; needles can wear out; decks can fail; power can go off. In fact, all electrical equipment will break at some point. Worse still, people can stop dancing.

So what do you do in these situations? Panic? No, you only panic if you are inexperienced. Experience tells DJs that problems can be solved. There are certain gremlins that crop up again and again. Knowing these and spotting them quickly means you can act fast and prevent those dancers from sitting down. Appendix 4 contains a quick guide to some of the main problems you may encounter in a live situation. Learn to spot them fast and know how to resolve them.

If things go wrong, stop, take some deep breaths and concentrate on working out what the problem is. It is likely to be fixable. Don't let people hassle you. If you can put a long tune on whilst you deal with whatever's wrong, do it. See if the manager or promoter can help you if possible, but be prepared to deal with the problem on your own. (See Appendix 4 for solutions to dealing with difficulties.)

Your ears

As a DJ, your ears are your business. Exposing them regularly to loud volumes will damage them. Damaged ears aren't much good to DJs and there are plenty of DJs who suffer from ear problems. Without protection you could get tinnitus which manifests itself as a permanent ringing in the ears. You could also go deaf.

The typical night club DJ plays music at around the 100 dB range. Listening to music at this level for more than two hours will have an impact on your ears and that's just music from the speakers. Headphone volumes have even more impact.

Noise-induced hearing loss is caused by damage to an organ in the ear called the cochlea. The tiny hairs and nerves on the cochlea are fragile and get damaged by high frequencies. When this happens there is a lower perception of volume.

Don't let this happen to you by protecting your ears. When exposed to loud music for long periods of time, as in a night club, take a break from the noise and go and have a chat in the chill-out room. Keep volume levels down when listening to music at home or on your MP3 player. Practise cueing and mixing at lower volumes. Turning the monitor down will help you do this.

Invest in some bespoke earplugs. Well made earplugs cut out the damaging higher frequencies whilst allowing you to hear the lower end of the music. You can therefore DJ with them without any problems. You could use cheap foam earplugs from a chemist but these will make the overall sound muffled. It's far better to spend the £100–£150 it costs to have a bespoke pair moulded to fit your ears which allow you to DJ. Many professional DJs do this. Ask someone to recommend an audiologist.

If you love music, respect your ears:

- Take a break from loud music.
- Don't listen to music at high volumes at home or on the move.
- Ask an audiologist to fit you with customised earplugs.
- Learn to cue and mix at lower headphone volumes.
- Turn the monitor down if you can.
- Leave your cueing headphone slightly off your ear to lessen the impact.
- Contact the RNID www.rnid.org.uk for advice if you start having hearing problems.

DJ etiquette

As well as respecting your ears, you should respect other DJs. It's obviously always a good thing to be friendly and polite. But it's also useful to know how to not annoy other DJs. It's rude to treat another DJ's music or equipment with disrespect. Treat your peers as you'd like to be treated. Follow the unsaid rules of DJ etiquette:

1 Be on time. Most DJs will be happy to carry on playing music, but being late is unprofessional and the outgoing DJ may have another gig they need to get to. By being early you also make sure you are not going to play a record the last DJ has recently played which is boring for the crowd.

2 Let the outgoing DJ know you have arrived and discuss when you are going on. Don't be anal about this. Be flexible if they want to play another record, let them. Be in the booth a tune or two before you are due to go on.

3 Let the last record from the DJ finish before you play. Don't cut to your music immediately when switching over.

4 Doing a power down on the warm-up DJ's last tune is slightly rude.

5 If warming up for another DJ, offer to move your record box to give the incoming DJ space in the booth.

6 Let the incoming DJ know of any problems with the equipment or sound. For instance, if the crossfader isn't working, let them know.

7 Don't get in the way of a DJ working in the booth.

8 Don't start talking to another DJ if they are in the middle of a mix.

9 If you are warming up for another DJ, you should bear in mind what they are likely to be playing when coming towards the end of your set. It's good for the dancefloor if you lead neatly into what they are going to be hearing next.

10 Don't chat up a DJ's girlfriend/boyfriend when they are working.

07

originality

In this chapter you will learn:
- how to develop your own style
- to be yourself
- where to find great music.

Being able to read a crowd and to programme a set that they will respond well to is at the very heart of DJing. If you are good at these and can mix effectively you really have what it takes to be a DJ.

However, being a competent DJ is pretty much a waste of time if you are playing the same music as most other DJs. DJing is about expressing a passion for music for others to enjoy. There is no point being a DJ if you are unoriginal. So what if you can do spinbacks and cuts if you play the same music as countless others?

The one thing the world is not short of is DJs. If you are going to stand out from your peers, you need to develop your own style. This is as much about music choice as it is technique. All accomplished, successful DJs have their own style and sound. Jeff Mills, 2ManyDJs, François Kevorkian, Felix Da Housecat, Gilles Peterson, DJ Cash Money, DJ Heather, Fatboy Slim, The Chemical Brothers, The Scratch Perverts, Mark Farina, Fabio, Phil Asher, Bjorn Türske, Rainer Trüby, Roni Size, Adam Freeland, Annie Nightingale, Basement Jaxx, Danny Tengalia, Sasha, Cutmaster Swift, Roger Sanchez, DJ Marky, Ivan Smagghe, Erol Alkan – they are all originals to name but a few. They all have one thing in common, they all sound like themselves.

Imagine a night of stand-up comedy at your local pub where the first comedian tells four good jokes and as a result manages to keep the crowd on his side. Then the second comedian begins his routine and tells two of the same jokes mixed in with two new ones. The crowd appreciate the new jokes but get a bit restless during the old ones. Then the final comedian stands on stage does exactly the same jokes as before but in a different order. What happens? The crowd boos him off. Why? Because copying others, however dressed up it is, is boring and uncreative. It goes against the very nature of entertainment.

Take risks and don't play safe. DJing should be a wild expression of passion, not a rehearsed and tame collection of predictable music. There are way too many DJs who all sound like one another.

So don't be DJ Sheep. Be your own DJ. Be DJ You. Be original.

Your style

A DJ is little more than the music he or she plays. The most skilled DJ on the planet is not going to have legions of fans if all they play is Italo-disco or electro. It might be your favourite type of music and you might be a true expert on the subject but you need to be accessible to audiences. It is only highly successful DJs who have the luxury of playing their chosen speciality night after night.

The key to forging your own style lies in developing your own tastes in music and making them accessible to different audiences. Never forget that it is about making people dance (unless you are a chill-out DJ!), not about showing off your rare collection of early rap tracks.

True music lovers will always naturally develop a taste for many different styles of music. You'd be hard pressed to find an electro-house DJ who didn't also appreciate the captivating qualities of techno, disco and even dub reggae, or a hip-hop DJ who didn't like funk, film soundtracks and a bit of rock. Having eclectic tastes is no bad thing. The broader your knowledge of music the better.

It is very useful to be versatile especially when starting out. The more gigs you can get, the more experience you gain. That means starting out by being competent enough to play a warm-up set in a club on Friday night, a friend's wedding on Saturday and a bar full of hungover people reading the papers on Sunday afternoon.

Increasingly DJs are basing their style on being eclectic, on mixing together numerous music styles in order to keep today's low-concentration audiences entertained. The DJ duo who founded the Ninja Tune label, Coldcut, helped make an art of this in the late '80s. For them it was all about playing great records whatever their style. For them DJing was all about trying to get from one record to the next.

At the same time it's worth being careful to be known for your style. A DJ whose brief is too wide could come across as bland. Your name is your brand and promoters need to know what that brand means. They don't want to book DJ J Bloggs to play a house set, if he turns up and spins hip-hop. Keep your style well-defined, whilst not ignoring other types of music. Your style is your musical trademark.

You can use digital technology to make your sound stand out too. Using programmes like Traktor or Ableton you can make your own re-edits. Alternatively, use the looping facilities that some mixers and CD decks have to add a dynamic and fun element to your sets.

Be sure to keep your style moving forward too. As with technology, music changes and develops. Dance music and hip-hop in particular constantly morph into new styles and sub-genres. Alongside this, shifts in culture mean that audiences' tastes change. UK club culture is a very different place now when compared to 1995, for example. Back then the acid-house explosion had given birth to hardcore, jungle, drum'n'bass, deep house, progressive house, techno and trip hop. In 1995 each of these sounds could be found on the dancefloors of Britain. Today you can find new forms of all these sub-genres alongside the likes of a bootleg culture, punk funk, funky house, electro house, chill-out, grime, R'n'B, ragga and trance to name but a few.

Keeping abreast of changes in music is second nature to music fans. As a DJ, you should always strive to make sure your box is full of fresh tunes. DJs need to have an intimidating grasp of music history but also a second sense of what is about to happen on the dancefloor and in the studio.

To summarise, the music you choose to play should come from your heart. It should be the music you love. But don't be afraid to explore the perimeters around that music and to even dip your toes into other genres. Being familiar with more music styles gives you more knowledge. Owning more styles of music makes you a more versatile DJ and gives you more ammunition in your fight to make that dancefloor groove. Don't be afraid to mix styles up. It makes for a great night rather than another case of 'I've heard it all before'. For instance, if you love vocal or funky house music, why not try deep house or electro house? If you like house music per se, why not discover its roots and listen to disco and electro? Stay ahead of the competition by buying new and old music. You could soon find that your thrilling sets become your trademark.

Relying on big tunes

All DJs have their secret weapons. The big tunes that never fail to make the dancefloor go crazy. These should be kept and treasured and used at the right moment to take a crowd to another level.

These big tunes should be tracks you have discovered over the years, new or old, that preferably are not heard all over national radio. The best secret weapons in your box are the tunes that help make your sets unique. Not the same big records that are number 1 in every big-name DJ's chart that week.

There are three golden rules when it comes to playing big tunes:

1 Make your big tunes as unique to you as you can. By all means play the latest killer anthem, but also develop your own personal anthems. Do you really want to sound like every other DJ?
2 Play them at the right moment and at the right time.
3 Don't rely on them and definitely don't base your set solely around them.

I was once asked to help judge a DJ competition. On the opening night three DJs played three very different sets. The first one played a competent, well-structured warm-up set that got the night going and slowly helped pack the dancefloor. The second DJ played a terrible racket with lousy mixing. And the third was a girl who brought at least 20 friends who immediately surrounded the booth and went mad as she played anthem after anthem after anthem. She had her friends dancing, but she didn't go through to the next round. The warm-up DJ did. DJ number three might as well have put on a 'Now That's What I Call Dance Anthems' CD. She banged out her anthems at deafening volume. She may have had the attention of the dancefloor, but in terms of the DJ competition, the judges all agreed the warm-up DJ had shown the most promise by thinking about what the floor and time required. He had not relied on big tunes and it paid off.

Building a collection

Believe it or not, a DJ's record collection is more important than his decks. Why? Well, clubs and bars have decks but not records. Or, put more blatantly, your music is more important than your equipment and even more important than your mixing ability. DJing isn't about mixing. It's about dancing. And however hot your beat juggling skills are, you simply won't cut it if your tunes are poor.

Even if your music is good, you need a lot of it. A couple of boxes of records and the knowledge of how to put them together still does not mean you will be a successful DJ. You need a collection. A library to choose moods from. A library to pluck atmospheres, classics, rare gems and fantastic beats from.

Music is truly an international language and your records are your vocabulary. There is no point learning the grammatical structure of a language (i.e. mixing) without the words (the tunes) to embellish it. Similarly there is no reason to learn to sing without lyrics. Likewise there is no point learning to mix without building a substantial and in-depth collection.

Real DJs are always looking for more tunes. A record collection can never be complete. That is part of the attraction. You may have all the rap classics from past and present, but what about the funk, disco and soul that hip-hop took its first breaks from?

I've seen one of New York's hardest working DJs Danny Krivit spending all his free time whilst over in London for a gig record shopping. I mean five to six hours in one record shop then on to the next. He's been DJing since the 1970s, yet he's still obsessed with finding more music. Years later I was to find the true extent of this obsession when I was invited to interview him at his apartment on Lower East Manhattan. I was expecting an impressive collection but nothing prepared me for the size of his music stash. Practically every single wall was lined with records bar the bathroom. There were piles of vinyl and CDs all over the floor right up to his bed. I told him that this had to be the largest collection I had come across yet. He said it was nothing; he had two storage lock-ups as well.

Hopefully you won't need to pay for storage space for your music collection. But be warned: music, especially record collections, can take over your home. There is a good argument for keeping all the music you ever own. You never know when your taste might change or when an old record you haven't played for years suddenly sounds really great again.

On the other hand amassing a decent-sized collection inevitably means there will be some CDs or 12″s that you aren't likely to use again. This is less of a problem with CDs and definitely not a problem with digital audio files, but a record collection is physically very bulky. It could be a good idea once or twice a year to go through your collection, make some hard choices and whittle out the tunes that were useful in their day but unlikely to be spun again. You can take these to your local second-hand dealer (some will even come to you if you have enough to sell) and exchange them for other tunes or put the money towards those all-important new headphones.

The reality is you need a collection that will arm you for any circumstance or occasion. DJs' collections are often divided up by genre so they know where to find those soul and pop 12"s for their mate's wedding, the cutting-edge electronic music CD-Rs for that gig in a warehouse in Berlin and the roots reggae 7" singles for a summer's afternoon at a beach bar. Go in deep and collect a wide variety.

Finding and buying the music

Rather than perfecting mixing or actually DJing, a DJ will spend most of their time searching for new music. The good news is, it is now easier to source good music than ever before. The internet has brought record shopping to you whether you live in a tower block, forest or cave. For a full list of recommended online and offline shops see Chapter 12: 'Taking it further'.

Where to buy music:

- High street chains
- Independent record shops
- Second-hand record shops
- Record fairs
- Charity shops/car boot sales
- Online shops
- Legal download music stores.

High street chains

The mainstream high street stores are fine for chart hits but not for much else. Some larger HMVs and Virgin Megastores have decent dance sections that are always worth browsing in, but you can't always listen to the music before purchase.

Independent record shops

For more underground music you are going to have to dig deeper. This is where independent record shops really help. If you live in a large city you should be well serviced with independent stores specialising in all genres of music. By supporting your independent record retailer you will be helping keep that shop, the independent record labels stocked within and the independent music scene alive. What's more, if you visit regularly you are likely to get a level of service you won't find at the major chains. DJs rely on switched-on record shop staff telling them which tracks are really hot each week. The staff at a good record shop will get to know your tastes, suggest tracks you hadn't considered and even put stuff aside for you so that it's waiting for you when you next come in. It can pay to visit these shops during quiet periods rather than on Friday evenings or Saturday afternoons when DJ Large and his mates have all the staff's attention.

Some shops though may well try to push tunes on to you that you don't need. So remember to be wary unless you have a well-established relationship with the staff. Never buy anything without listening. Any decent shop will have listening decks although second-hand shops tend not to. It's worth hearing tunes you are seriously considering buying at least twice. It's amazing how quickly a small pile of CDs or vinyl can add up. Make sure you are a discerning buyer. Ask yourself if it's really good. Will it fit what you play? Will it work on the dancefloor?

Second-hand record shops

Remember to check out the second-hand shops as well as the new. It is often here you will discover that hard-to-find Mantronix 12" or Masters At Work production. Most unfortunately don't have record or CD players for you to use so do your research first. If you know what you are looking for, these shops can be treasure troves. Some may over-price rare records, so check out how much certain tracks usually cost. You also need to be extra careful about checking the damage to vinyl. Unless mint, second-hand records will be scratched and marked to some degree.

Some second-hand shops may have a service that allows you to tell them which tunes you are after by giving them a wish list. This is really useful because they will email or call you when that tune comes in.

You can obviously off-load old tunes at these shops too. In fact many DJs do this, especially those making the transition from vinyl to CD or MP3. Ask the manager if they are due to get any large record collections coming in soon. If so, be ready to pounce.

Record fairs

Record fairs are massive second-hand music markets where serious dealers, usually with long hair and beards, gather to flog their wares in dusty old halls. You can often find forthcoming fairs advertised in the back of *NME* or *Record Collector*. Expect more rock records than dance, but worth a nose nevertheless. These are happy hunting grounds for the intrepid DJ, but it's probably best not to take your partner unless he or she is a collector too.

Charity shops/car boot sales

Many a producer has found great samples from records in charity shops. Always worth a look for that ultra-cheap bargain, but also often cleaned out by the DJ before you. Car boot sales may be a better bet if you can be bothered to wade through the chintz. Because the records you will find here will be so cheap, you can afford to take risks on what you are buying.

Online shops

Most record shops now have online shops too so it is always worth using these if you don't live near a particularly good shop or haven't got the time to go. There are hundreds of mail-order services too. Make sure you can hear samples before you buy where possible, and as with all internet transactions be aware of online fraud. Only buy from secure sites. For a list of good online stores see Chapter 12: 'Taking it further'.

Legal download music stores

There are a number of excellent online stores that specialise in classic back-catalogue or cutting-edge legal music downloads. Again, listen before you buy but also make sure you are getting decent-sized music files. Any file with a bit rate at 128kbps is likely to sound poor on a big club system. Better to buy files at a higher bit rate such as 192kbps, 256kbps or better still 320kbps. For a list of recommended download stores see Chapter 12: 'Taking it further'.

It's important not to waste your money whilst finding music that is going to give your sets the edge they need.

The main rules of hunting for music are:

1 Don't be tempted to buy something you haven't heard

Just because an artist made a great tune last month, doesn't mean their next one is going to be as good. Listen to everything you buy. If buying online, listen to the samples a few times until you are sure.

2 Be ruthless with yourself

You probably don't need/won't use all the records in the pile you have plucked. Do you really need every tune?

3 Tunes can sound very good in a shop, but lousy at home

Scientists are baffled as to why, but it's incredible how often you can get home and be disappointed by a track you bought that sounded great on the shop system. This is probably something to do with DJs getting all excited when they walk into a shop full of gleaming new vinyl and shiny little discs. Stay discerning.

4 Check the condition of vinyl

Don't buy vinyl that is scratched or warped. Don't take the copy everyone has been listening to to the till; ask for a new, shrink-wrapped one.

5 Build rapport with the staff at the best local stores

This way you're unlikely to miss any crucial releases.

6 Keep receipts

DJs can claim the costs of records against tax.

7 When buying downloads use legal shops that specialise in cutting-edge music and offer high-quality files such as 192kbps, 256kbps or 320kbps

This way you keep within the law and avoid poor quality music.

The dedicated DJ will always be on the look out for great new music. It pays to read the music press, looking at the reviews and DJ charts to see which records are being recommended. DJs' 'favourite records ever' charts are particularly good. Similarly, shops will often have their own in-store charts that the enthusiastic staff have fought over. Keep an eye on these for tunes you might have missed.

Radio is another key source for discovering new music. Specialist (usually late-night) shows play the more interesting tunes. Check their websites for track listings.

Likewise, internet radio and podcasts are great places to hear other recommendations and learn about new genres.

Hanging out and chatting in independent shops can be really useful for networking and meeting promoters. Plus, online music forums can be good for tip-offs on tunes and for virtually meeting fellow music fanatics.

08

turning pro

In this chapter you will learn:
- how to get paid bookings
- how to work as a
  professional
- how to be sent music for free
- how to approach radio
  stations.

Starting out and getting booked

If your goal is to become a working DJ you need to gain as much experience and contacts as possible. That means it is a good idea to take any paid and unpaid bookings at first. Getting your name about, meeting people involved in the club and music industries, and good solid experience is crucial to developing into a skilled and paid DJ.

Developing all the technical skills you need at home still won't fully prepare you for cutting it in a club or even a bar environment. Dealing with promoters, different audiences, bad sound systems are all things you learn to deal with through experience (see Chapter 06: 'The dancefloor' for advice on how to handle such situations). But how do you get experience? How do you get booked?

Once you are happy that you are at a good enough standard of technical and programming ability, you have a thorough understanding of what makes a crowd tick, and you are the proud owner of a respectable music collection, you are ready to go after as many bookings as you can get. There are a number of things that you can do to help you get these bookings. By always following this advice you will give yourself a better chance of convincing promoters and venue owners that you are the one they need to make sure their punters keep on coming back for more.

Making a demo mix

The first thing you are going to need to help you get booked is a demo mix. If a promoter hasn't had the chance to check you out whilst playing live, they will request a demo mix. Your demo mix needs to be put on to a CD-R to make it easy for promoters to listen to. It is also worth making sure you make your demo following these guidelines:

Make the demo reflect your style

Be true to your taste. Don't try to do anything too flash. The music needs to fit the night that the promoter is running.

Don't worry about small errors

The promoters you are sending it to are unlikely to be
accomplished DJs themselves. The odd glitch is unlikely to be
noticed. It's much more important to have really good tunes on
there that make people want to dance. So if you make the odd
hiccup in the mix, it is probably best to ignore it rather than
redo the entire mix which obviously takes time. Unless the mix
is rotten, you can probably get away with it. It's the tunes that
count.

Programme the demo well

You have time to think carefully about what you are going to
play. Make sure the opening track is a real attention grabber
and establishes the mood perfectly. I've heard many demos over
the years that start with a loud, over-exposed, peak-time club
anthem. Don't start with these – it sounds awful. Build the mix
in a clever way. It could be worth doing a clever a cappella mix
or playing a great old tune as a surprise or even a non-dance
record to stir things up. Make sure you also leave on a good
note. That final track could be the one the promoter always
remembers you by.

The mix should be somewhere between 40–70mins long

That's enough time to demonstrate a concise, well thought out
short set.

Keep an eye on your levels when recording your mix

You don't want the demo to be too quiet or too loud or, worse
still, you don't want it distorting in places. Make sure you stay
out of the red on the output levels on your mixer by setting the
output at a prudent level. Constantly check the levels on the
device you are recording with and make adjustments on the
input volume whenever necessary, making sure you stay away
from the red whilst having a strong enough signal to get
reasonable sound levels.

Make sure your demo disk is well presented

Don't leave the cover and disk blank. Make sure its looks professional. These days it is easy to print off a respectable looking cover and CD label. Have your name and contact details clearly printed on both the cover and CD. It might be an idea to have a regular logo you use on all your demos to give them some personality. Giving the demo a date indicates how old the mix and therefore the music is.

Make new demos every two months or so

It's good practice and keeps your music up to date.

How to get booked

The competition from other DJs is fierce. Once you have made lots of copies of your marvellous demo, you need to get as many people involved in clubs and music to hear it as possible. You also need to be very visible.

Tell everyone you know that you are available

You never know when a friend of friend is throwing a party and needs a DJ.

Hang around record shops

Network with people who live and breathe club and music culture. Or better still, get a job in a record shop. You'll be meeting promoters and other DJs in a flash.

Be prepared to take any gig

It doesn't matter that it is a small bar, pub, wedding or birthday party. It's all good experience that brings you closer to your goal. If you are a student ask the union's entertainments staff if they have any gigs available.

Target any bars or clubs you would like to play at

Start off by targeting local venues before going further afield. Send a mix CD together with a short, courteous letter with your contact details telling the manager that you are available. Make sure you research the venue beforehand. Don't send them a drum'n'bass mix if that venue only ever plays house.

Be prepared for knock backs

You might not get the response you were looking for, if you get one at all. Don't give up. Take it on the chin and look for the next gig.

Always carry a demo mix CD with you

You never know when you might bump into someone looking for DJs when you are in clubs, record shops or even at a gig performing. This is your calling card.

Promote your own night

If all else fails you could think about promoting your own night. That way you are sure to be booked. Bear in mind though it is hard work promoting a night successfully. Your main priority is to fill the venue, so it's probably best to start off small. Ask other DJs to bring their own crowds. Make sure the punters enjoy themselves. This is a great way of quickly building a reputation for a night with a difference. That reputation will reflect on you and lead to other bookings.

Enter DJ competitions

Look at magazines and flyers for news of DJ competitions being held in bars and clubs in your local area or on the radio. You will be up against other competitive hopefuls so be prepared to shine. These are great for gaining experience and you can ask the judges for feedback. The prizes are often DJ equipment or, better still, some regular bookings.

Get a job in the industry

It's never easy to get a job in the music industry. Jobs are advertised in *Music Week* – the industry's trade magazine – and on sites like www.uk.music-jobs.com. Starting out with work experience is often a good idea as this can lead to paid work. Once you have your foot in the door you should meet people able to help you find DJ work.

Make music

If you are making hot dance records you are almost guaranteed to get DJ bookings. Your tracks work as a calling card. If people have heard your sound on vinyl they will have a good idea of whether you'd fit into their night or not. The hotter your music is the more you can charge too.

How to stay booked

Once you have managed to secure that valued gig at a bar or club you obviously would like to get rebooked, turning it into regular work. Performing well and getting a terrific response from the crowd is blatantly the key to this. However, it is worth remembering that being as professional as possible also helps build a good relationship with the promoter or venue manager.

Be on time

Don't arrive late. It is rude and unprofessional. If you are stuck in traffic, let the promoter know as soon as you can. Arriving early gives you the advantage of soaking up the atmosphere and talking to the DJ who is on before you who might have some tips.

Be nice

Don't pester people, but do be polite and enthusiastic when meeting resident DJs, promoters or managers. A good rapport will help you get more work. Being friendly is always good for business.

Keep your record box up to date

Stay on top of musical trends and make sure your music doesn't sound tired. You should be searching for new music every week or two.

Be prepared to travel

Take gigs wherever they are. The more you make a name for yourself the more bookings you will receive from further afield.

Learn from your experiences

If you made mistakes at the last gig, think through why that was. What went wrong? How can you avoid it next time? If you got an amazing reaction think about why that gig went so well. What was the crowd responding to in particular? Which records sent them crazy?

Develop your own sound

Stand out from the countless other DJs be perfecting your own sound. Dare to be different by using your own re-edits of tracks. Don't copy other DJs. Have self-belief and learn to express yourself through your sets.

Keep flyers or press cuttings with your name on

These can be sent to other promoters to demonstrate that you are in demand and experienced.

Stay healthy

DJing isn't the healthiest profession in the world. It's full of late nights, long-distance travelling and very loud music. DJs are usually very tired people. Drink and drugs are never far away in the world of night clubs either. To stay enthusiastic, eager and professional, and to be able to cope with the physical demands of the job, you need to look after yourself or face burning out. Sleeping well, eating well, exercising and not giving in to temptation will help you cope with the lifestyle and keep you raring to go.

Getting paid

Competition from other DJs willing to step into your shoes is ever present. What's more, the club scene as a whole is getting less admissions than it did in the '90s. These two facts combined mean that DJ wages are probably falling, or at least static, rather than rising in the current climate. However, that doesn't mean you should not get paid if the venue you are playing at is making good money. Everyone starting out will do gigs for free whilst they are getting established. But once you are working regularly you should expect to get paid.

Wages vary dramatically depending on your reputation and where you are playing. Big-name DJs can easily expect to pull in anywhere between £800–£5000 or more a gig depending on the size of the gig they are playing. A venue such as The Ministry of Sound can pull in thousands of paying punters and will therefore pay good money to have big-name DJs to attract an audience. Playing in medium-sized venues as a working DJ you could expect to be paid somewhere between £200–£600 per night. In a bar you might earn along the lines of £50–£250. When playing in a pub you'd be doing well to earn £50–£100.

In the murky world of night clubs there are undoubtedly some slippery characters. It's therefore always a good idea to try and get paid upfront if possible and only with cash in hand. Some festivals or large organisations may want to pay you by cheque, but on the whole cash will be paid out, usually after you finish playing.

You may well be asked to provide an invoice. This means there is a paper trail that the tax man can follow. If you are earning money through DJing you should always declare it. DJs, like all entertainers, are on the Inland Revenue's radar. Remember to keep your receipts so you can claim tax against your expenses. Permitable expenses include: music, DJ equipment, computer equipment, travel, petrol, hotels, magazines, stationery, phone bills. These are all tax deductible so always remember to keep the receipts.

If you are travelling a long distance to a gig it is reasonable to ask the promoter to cover the cost of your hotel. Flights abroad to gigs should be covered too as part of your booking deal. Don't expect promoters to cover your travelling expenses in the UK though.

To avoid any unpleasant financial disagreements it is a good idea to have a legal contract drawn up. Smaller venues won't normally do these and it's probably best not to push for one. But for appearances at large events or established club nights or trips abroad you are best advised to have a contract.

Once you are working regularly it is important you know how much you are worth as a DJ, i.e. your market value. The fee you command should be realistic but reflect your ability to pull in punters to a venue.

If you are doing well and earning good money and you are in demand, it is a good idea to be flexible on your fee if you can.

Stay true to the music and the scene you love. If you are earning a lot from big club nights why not be flexible enough to offer your services at a reduced rate for a smaller, more underground venue, whose budget is far smaller? You will build a bond and gain respect from promoters and fans for this. A really healthy example of this attitude comes from the ground-breaking Optimo club in Glasgow. Residents JD Twitch and JG Wilkes have been in huge demand across Europe for the last couple of years due to their genre-bending sets that mix up electronic music with the likes of raw rock from The Stooges. They have taken many bookings but they have refused to follow the industry norm of milking every gig for what they can get. Their website states:

'We think DJs charging huge fees or being inflexible about their fees is ridiculous as it means some of the smaller, more interesting clubs aren't able to book the DJs they would like to have play. We do this for a living but playing a great club is more important to us than getting a huge fee. If you have a large budget and a full club, we expect to be paid accordingly but if you don't and would like us to come and play, get in touch and we will come to some arrangement. As there are two of us, it is also possible to book one of us to come if this makes it more affordable for you.

Optimo – striving to break down the bullshit that exists in DJ culture since 1997.'

This fantastic attitude not only means you are more likely to be able to hear these exciting DJs in action, but that they are helping to keep underground club culture alive. Without underground club culture there would be more boring clubs playing commercial music and fewer exciting records. In fact, without underground club culture there would be no hip-hop, house music, drum'n'bass, grime or techno! DJs need to help nuture underground music. It's not just about chasing the big bucks.

So, to recap:

- You need to be paid for your work.
- Know your market value.
- Be realistic about what you charge.
- Try to get cash in hand upfront.
- Declare your earnings to the tax man.
- Save all receipts for expenses.

- Make sure the promoter covers your travel and accommodation costs if playing abroad.
- Get a contract drawn up to avoid disagreements.
- Be flexible and help support smaller clubs as well as bigger ones.

Getting a booking agent

Booking agents can be very useful. Not only can they help secure you more gigs, they can bargain for higher fees and will set up contracts for you. They usually also acquire 50 per cent of the booking fee as a deposit for each gig they secure which protects you against cancellations. On top of this they will make necessary travel arrangements, booking accommodation, flights, drivers, visas and work permits.

For such great service they will take between 10–20 per cent of each booking fee they secure. However, agents won't just take anyone onto their books. They will only look at people who are going to make them money. They will know the market very well and will have a very good idea of how many gigs they will be able to get you.

An agency is unlikely to take you on unless you are making music, or have a high-profile radio show, or are attracting crowds within a particular genre. They will be looking for someone whose career they can nurture and develop.

If you are lucky enough to get taken on by an agent expect them to push up your price. If they look after you exclusively you should be able to come to an arrangement, giving your agent a slightly lower percentage. If you are exclusive with one agent they will look after your entire diary for you. You might however want to go with more than one agent in the hope of getting as many gigs as possible. This could be useful if you are able to play two different styles of music. Agencies will often have a reputation for certain styles just like clubs do. Yet you are likely to feel a bit unloved unless you commit to one agency.

Be wary though if you are a small name at a large agency – you may not get the attention you deserve as the agents may concentrate on pushing the big guns who command the high fees. If you aren't a name DJ it may pay off to turn your attention away from the large, national DJ agencies and look towards more local operations. Local agencies will expect you to be hard-working and flexible (i.e. to accept a last-minute booking without complaint). In return they will strive to connect you with local venues, usually bars and clubs. Be warned though, this might mean playing to more commercial audiences – crowd pleasers and chart hits at the ready.

It's also worth bearing in mind that agents aren't managers. They won't babysit you if you are having a mid-life crisis or have had your car stolen. That's part of the fun of being a manager ...

Getting a manager

As with booking agents, there isn't much point getting a manager early on in your career as a DJ. Like an agent they will take a percentage of your earnings. Your name as a DJ has to be on the rise to make it worthwhile. Whilst an agent will champion you to promoters, a manager will use their music industry contacts to get you work putting together compilations or doing remixes or recordings. They will also look after your PR and give practical advice on your career.

There is no reason why you can't manage your self though. At least you can be trusted to have your own interests at heart.

Getting on mailing lists

Record companies often either run in-house club promotions departments or use external club promotions agencies to help them get their records played to as many people in clubs as possible. In other words, record companies are keen to help market their music by getting DJs to play it.

People working in club promotion will be given batches of each relevant new release to send out to the DJs on their mailing lists. These mailing lists are divided up by geographical region, DJs' tastes and how important certain DJs are to certain scenes, e.g. Gilles Peterson is going to be very high up on the promotional mailing lists for jazz and soul dance music.

DJs who are on a mailing list will get sent new 12"s and CDs before the music is released. Unfortunately, that doesn't mean the music is any good. In fact, many copies of records you may get sent will appear at your local second-hand record shop. If you think about it, great records are going to need far less promotion that poor ones. Hence highly average records often get big club promotion pushes.

The people who send you the music will usually enclose a reaction sheet for you to fax or email back. This is where you say what you thought of the record and how the crowd responded. It's a chore filling these in but part of the deal. You're likely to be removed from the mailing list if you fail to react. Some club promotion departments such as EMI now allow you to do this online which makes it quicker and easier.

You do sometimes receive some good stuff too. It's worth being on the lists to know what's coming out and, more importantly, to know what everyone else is playing. But if you build up a good reputation for your style of music and are friendly and responsive to the people running the lists, you may well find yourself being sent very limited, hot new tracks that they will count on you to help break.

To get on to mailing lists you will be asked to prove that you are regularly DJing or hosting a radio show. You may be asked to send in flyers with your name on as proof. Persevere with trying to convince them to put you on the list if you are rejected at first. Let them know about all the new gigs you are playing.

The most essential thing to learn about mailing lists though is not to play the music you receive from them exclusively. That's exactly what everyone else is doing. You need your own sound so go shopping for those special *you* sounds.

Small independent record labels may not be able to afford to do large mailouts of their releases, but some will. They may run their own list or use club promotion specialists to do it for them. It could be worth contacting labels you particularly want to support directly and asking them politely if they have a mailing list. Otherwise you could contact the specialists listed in 'Taking it Further'. Only get in touch with specialists who deal with your style of music and be prepared to convince them you should be included. Don't lie to them. You will be found out and it's unprofessional as well as dishonest.

A list of key club promotions companies can be found in Chapter 12: 'Taking it further'.

Playing on the radio

DJing on the radio is a very different proposition to playing in clubs. In clubs it is a DJ's job to keep people dancing. On radio, DJing has nothing to do with dancing. It is about keeping people listening and coming back for more. As a radio presenter you may inspire people to dance around their radio sets at home, but this isn't the main focus.

Instead, radio is about presentation rather than performance. As a radio jock it is your job to provide a well-structured collection of music which is presented in a dynamic and captivating way, perhaps with interviews, competitions or news pieces interspersed within the show.

In fact, many DJs find they really enjoy radio after years of cutting it on the dancefloor. Its very nature means you are not bound by the rules of the dancefloor. In other words you don't have to play just dance music. It is a fun and rewarding opportunity to play a variety of genres and tempos. Obviously you can talk about or discuss the music too. What's more, radio gives you a chance to communicate to very large audiences as well as the chance to receive useful feedback from your listeners.

There are many different styles of radio programmes and presentation. There are commercial pop shows; talk shows; specialists shows that focus on new music; and club shows that concentrate on DJs providing mixes. Different shows require different skills but all radio presenters need to be interesting enough to hold listeners. They also need to be confident enough not to be nervous. They should of course also have a clear voice and not be prone to swearing or pausing, er, mid-sentence.

As a radio DJ you will usually work in a team with an engineer who runs the studio and looks after the signal quality, and a producer who manages the programme helping you to create a running order, and to handle interviewees and guests. Most of the hard work is down to you though. Radio presenting is a very hands-on job. You need to be good at using the microphone, cueing music, playing jingles or adverts, taking calls, dealing with competitions, linking to news or outside broadcasts and obviously controlling the many different sound sources on the studio desk.

On top of this it is likely that you'll need to know how to get the sound levels right and how to programme the show often using the station's comprehensive programming software. One crucial skill worth acquiring is learning how to edit shows using software such as Pro-tools. This gives you the ability to make your show sound very slick with great segues between the music and words.

There are unquestionably numerous and varied radio stations. If you have your heart set on radio presenting you need to target the right kind of station. You will need to put together a well-made, slick showcase CD to send stations' Programme Directors. They are the people responsible for recruiting new presenters. It's best to chop the music down and concentrate on your presentation style. It needs to be very convincing, natural and full of great links.

Your show CD should then be sent to the stations with your CV and contact details attached. Think about which stations would be right for you. Student radio is a great way for many radio jocks to start. Ask your union about student-run shows or contact the Student Broadcast Network. Some universities and colleges will have permanent broadcasting licenses whilst others may operate on temporary licenses broadcasting for a month at a time. These temporary licenses may also be granted to local communities.

Hospital radio has always been a breeding ground for new talent despite its cheesy image. Like student radio, it is a great place to offer your time in exchange for experience.

Pirate radio is a natural home for many club DJs. Judge Jules, Gilles Peterson and John Peel all started out on the pirates. Pirate stations got their name in the 1960s because it was illegal to broadcast on land as they were not licensed. The stations, such as Radio Caroline, operated at sea, broadcasting from boats in the English Channel and North Sea. Pirate radio has always been associated with playing new and underground music. The same is still true, with hundreds of stations around the UK playing many different genres of music. London pirate stations play a central role in many music scenes, including grime, but you will also find plenty of house, ragga, reggae, and drum'n'bass.

The illegal status of pirate radio means that it isn't always easy get to involved and to host your own show. Although some of the stations are run by genuine enthusiasts, there are plenty of shady characters operating too. The stations themselves are usually, but not always, based in disused flats in tower blocks. Staying one step ahead of the law is always a priority so you may well be halfway through a show when you have to make a sharp exit.

I used to host a weekly show in Sheffield every Thursday. I remember doing one show in particular at yet another new flat (the venue seemed to change every three or so weeks). Having finished the show I went from the bedroom where the decks and equipment were through to the empty living room only to find a dead dog riddled with maggots in the middle of the room. Such a charmed life is to be expected in pirate radio.

The transmitters for pirate stations are usually on top of separate blocks from where the broadcasting takes place in order to prevent the authorities capturing the rest of the equipment. I know of one station based in a farmyard barn in the heart of Epping Forest. The power was siphoned off the adjacent M25 motorway whilst the show was transmitted to London via a tower block in Tottenham.

Whilst it may sound glamorous, it isn't. It's a great way to showcase the music you love to fellow music fans but the fact is it is illegal. The Department of Trade and Industry has the responsibility of policing the airwaves. Their detection equipment can easily pinpoint transmitters. You can get fined up to £1000 and have all your equipment and music seized.

The BBC runs training programmes and has many local radio stations which are excellent places to start out for the eager professional. Have a look at the BBC's radio trainee scheme at www.bbc.co.uk/newtalent.

Increasingly, the internet is a great source of radio. Many radio shows can be found online with countless stations dedicated to the specialist genres, e.g. www.ministryofsound.com/radio or www.radiomagnetic.com. If you are really dedicated and have a techy friend who can help, why not launch your own internet radio station? Be prepared to give up your social life though. Alternatively, send in a demo to see if you can do a show on an internet radio station.

For further info see Chapter 12: 'Taking it further'.

09

what the
DJs say

In this chapter you will learn:
- what makes some of the world's leading DJs tick
- which formats they recommend
- what were their best and worse moments as DJs
- what advice they want to give you.

Every DJ has different experiences, preferred techniques, tricks or stories to share and tell. Here some of the world's leading DJs, the real pros, give you an insight into their working lives as well as invaluable advice on what it takes to become a master of the craft.

Tom Findlay, Groove Armada

DJ style: House to block party beats

Can be heard at: Space, Ibiza; Lovebox, London

What's the best thing about DJing?

For me it's indulging a love of music. I'm always out there hunting for fresh tunes. And then from time to time, maybe one night in four, you do get this thing when DJing can be quite beautiful and you have a lovely crowd, and you all sort of 'commune', and they love the music that you love and you in turn love them. Mostly though it's well paid, but with that comes a bit of soul destruction – late nights driving home in cars wondering whether you're too old for this!

Two really useful mixing tips?

1 If it's all going 'Pete Tong' never just pull out of a mix, the crowd will respect you more if you fight your way through the hebegeebees.

2 When mixing, I always have the track to be mixed in a few decibels lower than the one playing, with a bit of the bass cut. This allows you to work it in nice and slow.

Do you use Final Scratch or Ableton Live? What do you think of this new technology?

I have used it as a demo. It's brilliant technology, really ingenious and in time will bring more people into DJing, as ultimately vinyl is pretty pricey. But as it stands I am vinyl and CD only.

What's the worse disaster that has happened to you whilst DJing?

Definitely DJing in Ibiza a little the worse for wear. I kept enjoying the tunes that I was cueing on the headphones so much that I forgot to actually bring them in front of house. So consequently I kept looking up to see a room of people staring at me in total silence. I did it about six times. What a wally.

What advice would you give an aspiring DJ?

DJ for girls not boys.

Jon Moore and Matt Black, Coldcut (founders of the Ninja Tune label)

DJ style: Wildly eclectic; everything from breaks to hip-hop to electronica

Can be found at: Solid Steel nights, worldwide; Solid Steel internet radio shows

What's the best thing about DJing?
Seeing loads of people all with massive grins, totally on the same groove.

Two really useful mixing tips?
1 BPM all your tunes, i.e. work out the mean tempo. As a rule hip-hop is 88bpm to 110 bpm; house, garage, breakbeat, disco are all around 118bpm to 135 whilst jungle is 150bpm to 180bpm.
2 Use the master tempo on CDJ–1000 all the time so you can really nudge a tune hard to keep it in time, without getting a big pitch slur as you nudge. Excellent for mixing old irregular BPM tunes.

Do you mix with MP3s? Which format do you prefer?
We are not big fans of MP3s having played at Fabric in London and been able to compare. It's got to be CDs for new stuff, vinyl for the old stuff, and pure stereo WAVs at the best quality possible whenever possible.

Do you use Final Scratch or Ableton Live?
Ableton Live is our tool of choice for performance and composition. It is a development of earlier Coldcut ideas like My Littlefunkit and DJamm. Search for 'Coldcutter' for a free Live compatible VST plug-in we made that will funk any loop.

What is the future of DJing?
Digital jockeys will mix all media. Audiovisual adds images to the sound. To do it right in perfect sync see vjamm.com. Live cinema is the way forward. The DJ definition remixes itself to stay alive!

What's the worse disaster that has happened to you whilst DJing?
We played in Norway once in a gale on top of a big hill in the rain in between knees-up local bands with no sound check. The wind kept blowing the arm off the record. Our laptop got the hump and crashed. The next band sound checked over us and

we had no monitor. Our set was cut to 30 minutes thankfully. Somebody posted on our forum saying 'It was rubbish'. Boy, they were right!

What advice would you give an aspiring DJ?

Don't be needlessly far out. Yes, we do what we do, but it's good to meet the audience halfway. Once you've got people going with something well known you get their confidence and can then wig out more. The other way round can be painful. You are there for the people and yourself. Keep it balanced, don't worry if you clear the odd floor, e.g. coming on playing slower after banging house, they'll be back. Also there is valuable experience in every gig no matter its size. Perfect yourself ... have the ambition to become a master and know that it's a lifetime's work.

Fred Deakin, Lemon Jelly

DJ style: Eclectic and fun

Can be heard at: Benicasm festival, Spain

What's the best thing about DJing?

Connecting with a crowd of people through the power of music. On a good night there is no better place to be than behind the decks.

Two really useful mixing tips?

1 I'm still a big fan of turning off the turntable power and letting the record that's playing slow down gradually to a complete halt. It's a great way of turning the page if you're switching musical genres or tempos. I first saw Mark Moore do it at Heaven (Spectrum, I think) in the late '80s and it made the crowd go absolutely beserk.

2 The other one is what I call the 'crunch' mix – hitting the stop button on the upbeat and kicking off the next record on a downbeat. As you may gather I don't do a huge amount of beat mixing!

Which format do you prefer?

Vinyl is still my preference. I like to touch the music!

What's the worse disaster that has happened to you whilst DJing?

The first record I ever played in a club had dust on the needle and after a few seconds it went skating across the record making a terrible racket. With all eyes on me I tried to fade the previous record back in but all I got was silence. I hadn't realised that the turntable arm was up. The previous DJ had to show me. He gave me a record cleaner with the fierce instructions to use it. I put on New Order's Blue Monday which had just come out and it completely cleared the floor. I was then removed from the decks. I'm amazed I persevered.

What advice would you give an aspiring DJ?
To begin with take any gig you can because you'll always learn something. Your first goal is to find a crowd that loves to dance and play to them on a regular basis. Once you feel confident enough think about starting up your own night with some mates. It's much easier to evolve your style if the crowd has come along especially to hear you play. Always be nice to people asking for requests (unless they get rude first!) and if someone asks you to play a record that you have in your box then play it, otherwise why did you bring it? Finally remember this – if a DJ doesn't clear the floor at least once a night they are playing it far too safe.

Craig Richards, Fabric

DJ style: Underground house and techno

Can be found at: Fabric, London

What's the best thing about DJing?
Using the devil's music to excite and destroy vulnerable minds. Visiting London's parks during the week when no one is there and staying up late at the weekend.

Two really useful mixing tips?
1 Always stay one drink behind your audience.
2 Remember that talking about mixing is deeply uninteresting.

Do you use MP3s?
No, I do not use MP3s thank you very much but I've heard it's a new and exciting way of acquiring and sharing music. I'm resistant to anything that threatens the future of vinyl. I'm a creature of habit. I adore specialist record shops almost as much as I love pubs. I'm still romantically attached to vinyl. So much of my enjoyment of music involves touching and seeing records. Vinyl has a particularly special sound that I'm perfectly happy with.

Any DJ disasters?
Years ago at an illegal party I was told to turn the music off by
a very large angry bloke. Initially he had politely asked if we
would reduce the volume but in true acid house spirit we told
him to sod off. He left it a while then single-handedly stormed
the party wielding a carpenter's hammer. To this day I recall the
cold hammer against my forehead as he yelled at me. Apart
from that the only other disasters I recall are some of the utterly
disastrous sets I have played and I would like to take this
opportunity to apologise to anybody who has been
disappointed in me.

Any advice for aspiring DJs?
It's really all about the music. Seeking and finding new music is
an incredibly inspiring process but for me the juxtapositions
between old and new is where the excitement lies. Be
a selector and your enthusiasm for the music will be enough.
Make it your own and play it with love. Lastly a concept that
took me years to grasp – remain aware that consuming
alcohol in heroic quantity to combat the effects of stage fright
may compromise your performance.

Erol Alkan

DJ style: Indie rock to electro house

Can be found at: Trash, London

What's the best thing about DJing?
The point when you fully connect with everyone else in the
room. It's as intense as anything else I have ever experienced.
The travel, lifestyle, money and fame are all pretty low on the
list to be honest. I don't perceive myself as having that much of
those things.

Really useful mixing tip?
Avoid vocal lines clashing unless it's really clever, i.e. like some
type of call and response, such as one track asking a question
and the other giving an answer.

**Do you mix with MP3s? How does it compare to vinyl and
CDs? What's your preference?**
I do download MP3s, burn a CD and play it out, for sure. Most
of the new tracks I get are from producers or bands who are
emailing me their music. Obviously the sound quality is not as

good, but if you encode at 256kps then you have to really strain
to hear the difference. I can hear it a mile off as it is evident in
the reverb of the snare drum. MP3s seem to invade those certain
frequencies the most. I love playing off CD, but only using the
Pioneer CDJ–1000 Mk2s. I swear by them.

Do you use Ableton Live?
Ableton is extremely inventive and very powerful. The theories
and science of quantising beats and rhythms should be observed
if using this software – you may be able to mix stuff but make
sure the feel of the record doesn't suffer.

What advice would you give an aspiring DJ?
Only play music you love. Question every fad that comes before
you. Respect the DJs you love and not those who are merely
famous. It's your job to create an atmosphere; don't rely on
anyone else to do it. Finally, never bask in glory, it makes you
look like an idiot.

Miguel Migs

DJ style: Deep house

Can be found at: Mighty, San Francisco; El Devino, Ibiza

What do you enjoy about DJing?
I love entertaining and creatively turning people on to new
music.

Which formats do you use?
I mix CDs and vinyl. Both are great and with technology these
days mixing CDs is so similar to mixing vinyl.

What is the future for DJing?
There will always be people who want to go out and enjoy
listening to music while chilling at a bar or dancing at a club, so
I'm sure it will be around for a long time.

Any DJing disasters?
Whilst playing an outdoor venue in Turkey the army came
storming up, pointing machine guns at us screaming for us, to
stop the music in Turkish which I did not understand but it was
obvious what they meant. Apparently the promoters had no
permits or didn't pay off the right people so it ended there but
luckily we didn't go to prison or anything and still got paid, so
it wasn't so bad, I guess!

What advice would you give an aspiring DJ?

Stay true and passionate about the music. Don't start by expecting success or loads of money. Maybe that will come in time and maybe it will not, but have fun with it and enjoy it.

Pete Lawrence, The Big Chill

DJ style: Chill-out

Can be found at: The Big Chill festival or bar

What's the best thing about DJing?

Sharing music you feel passionate about with other people. Music is such a powerful mood manipulator and tool for altering brain chemistry. Its influence and power should not be underestimated!

What's the art of chill-out DJing?

Knowing and understanding the music you play counts for a lot, as a passionate DJ often translates to a receptive audience. Keep it varied, keep it engaging and take people on a journey.

Two really useful mixing tips?

1 Don't forget your headphones.
2 Pre-set checks: using CDJs, check the 'reverse' button isn't activated; check the varispeed is where you want it; and check all the EQs on the mixer.

Do you mix with MP3s?

I have recently started mixing totally with MP3s. A slight loss of sound quality (arguably inaudible to most ears) is more than made up for by being able to travel lightly with a laptop and a Hercules mixer, and to be able to carry an entire iTunes collection on a laptop. This technology is sure to develop fast.

What is the future for DJing?

More portable music via MP3s and DJing off computer. More environments where music not designed specifically for dancing can be played.

What's the worse disaster that has happened to you whilst DJing?

No one incident sticks out. I've played wrong tracks at the wrong speed (after years of listening to John Peel!). I've stopped the wrong record. I've turned up with CDs to find only vinyl turntables. At an early house party, in front of 800 people, I started a vinyl set mistakenly at +8! On New Year's Eve once, a very drunk woman once poured a pint over my head because I wouldn't come and deal with their request quickly enough!

What advice would you give an aspiring DJ?
Play music you feel, be honest to your own tastes and passions, not public expectations or trends. Be original, but pay attention to the DJs you most admire. Be organised. Seek out events and scenes and get to know the people involved in running them.

DJ Format

DJ style: Hip-hop

Can be heard at: Electric Picnic, Dublin or Leeds Festival

What's the best thing about DJing?
Taking music that you already enjoy and adding your own personal touch to it by mixing it with other music or scratching and cutting it up ... and hopefully improving it in the process.

Two really useful scratching tips?
1 Record yourself practising so you can listen back and get a better idea of how you sound.
2 Try to practise with other people so you can let someone else's style inspire you when you're sick of hearing your same old scratches.

What advice would you give an aspiring scratch DJ?
Just do it for yourself as a hobby. Don't expect to make a living or become some sort of star because you'll end up disappointed or not enjoying your DJing. Play records that you believe are good, don't just follow what everybody else is doing. Also in a club there is such a thing as too much scratching. Most scratch DJs don't know this!

What's your favourite type of gig?
Gigs where people appreciate the music being played and just want to dance and have a good time.

The Glimmers

DJ style: Underground dance music and forgotten gems

Can be heard at: Eskimo parties, Belgium

What do you love about DJing?
Blending different tracks by different artists together to make your own combinations. As a DJ you are in charge and you decide which tracks are played. In other words you decide how crazy the people can go.

Useful mixing tip?
Be patient, let the track do its work, then blend in the next one. Make sure that the tempo and the sound fits. Or make different and crazy combinations, but then you have to be skilled and fast.

How do you see DJing developing?
Systems like Ableton Live or Final Scratch will be more common in clubs and at festivals. But the DJ will have the same function of making a good selection, timing the tracks and being creative with the selection of those tunes.

Any funny DJ stories?
Once we were playing at a big party and Mo fainted in the middle of a mix when I was at the bar getting some fresh drinks. When I came back to the DJ booth, I saw Mo laying on the floor, and heard the two tracks playing and the people were going crazy to that mix. Very strange and scary.

What advice would you give an aspiring DJ?
Never give up, believe in yourself and make sure you are a bit different from the others.

Ewan Pearson

DJ style: Electro house

Can be found at: Kill The DJ, Paris

What's your favourite thing about DJing?
It's great introducing new music to people who haven't heard it yet. I love it when someone comes up and says, 'I didn't really think I liked this kind of music, but that was wicked ...'

Two really useful mixing tips?

1 When you're starting out just aim for short, neat segues. That's quite enough skill to be a decent DJ. Don't forget that quick, well-timed cuts in a disco style work fine too.

2 Don't worry too much about mixing. I think the most important factor with any DJ is selection: what you play, and the order in which you play it and how you present the music. Anything else is just window dressing. I'm not that bothered about technique. It's the destination that matters, not how you get there.

Do you mix with MP3s?

I do play MP3s but burned on to a CD. I only play high quality ones (192kbps as an absolute minimum) and I hassle promo companies to make stuff available at the highest bandwidth they can. You can hear a big difference between a low rate MP3 and a full 16-bit AIFF. As I make records myself I want the stuff I play to be heard at its best.

Do you use Final Scratch or Ableton Live? What do you think of this new technology?

I have yet to use either in a DJ situation. I would worry that Final Scratch would give too much programming choice and end up being confusing. I am intrigued to hear Sasha with his Ableton set-up. I hear amazing things about what he's doing and it seems to be the logical extension of his musical/harmonic mixing style. I have seen people like Twitch from Optimo play blazing sets using Live but I have yet to try it myself in public. I still have a sneaking fondness for boring old decks.

What advice would you give an aspiring DJ?

Try and find your own style. Make sure you're playing music that you love, rather than music that other people tell you is the next big thing. And if you can't get a gig, then start a night yourself. Don't wait to be discovered.

Trevor Nelson

DJ style: R'n'B

Can be heard at: Mercy, Norwich; Club Sanuk, Blackpool; BBC Radio 1

How is playing R'n'B different to other styles of mixing and DJing?

An R'n'B crowd is a healthy mix of male and female and not reliant on a hands in the air 'having it large' atmosphere. The music is slower than most so I would only be able to mix 50 per cent of my set; the rest is a combination of segues and blends.

What's the best gig you have done?

An MTV lick party in Dublin at The Temple Theatre for 2000 clubbers with impromptu live PAs from Missy Elliot, P. Diddy, Mariah Carey, Mary J. Blige, Whitney Houston, TQ, Bobby Brown and Lynden David Hall. The only act that was actually booked was The Honeyz.

Any DJing disasters?

Apart from taking the needle off the record while playing many times, during an outdoor gig in Athens the wind kept blowing the stylus off the vinyl for the first 20 minutes of my set which was a little embarrassing, especially as I was given a huge welcome before I played my first record.

Do you use the latest technology whilst DJing?

I am a vinyl man through and through. At most I may play 5 per cent of my set on CD but use no effects or digital wizardry at all.

How is club DJing different to radio?

Club DJing is instant gratification from the crowd; there are records that I play in clubs that really don't work on the radio. Radio for me is about songs and melodies and clubs are more about energy and production values.

Do you ever get nervous when DJing?

Sometimes, when I haven't played in a country before and I'm not sure if they will like what I'm going to play. The only other times are when there are DJs around me that I respect.

What was your big break into being a DJ?

My school disco was the first step at 18, but my real break was joining Kiss FM as a pirate DJ in 1985.

What advice would you give an aspiring DJ?

You must have passion first and no ulterior motives to DJ. It should feel like a hobby with no reward. If it becomes your living then try not to be too influenced by other DJs or else you'll never stand out from the crowd. Never be selfish when there is a crowd in front of you that you have to entertain.

Cosmo

DJ style: Deep soulful house to disco classics

Can be found at: The Loft parties, London or New York; Tenax, Italy

What's the best thing about DJing?
The best things about DJing are not having to do a real job, meeting other people who are just as obsessive about music as yourself and creating different sonic environments.

Three useful mixing tips?
1 Always preview the levels of your next track in cue to make sure they match the track you are playing before you start your mix.
2 Whilst you are mixing, adjust your EQ so that the frequencies of the two tracks do not clash. For instance, you may want to crossfade the bass while you are mixing.
3 Remember you don't always need to mix and can create more drama when not constantly playing at one continuous BPM.

Do you mix with MP3s? How do they compare to vinyl and CDs?
I don't work with MP3s because the sound quality is seriously degraded. I do work with CDs (the sound quality of which is degraded, as well, but not as much as MP3s) but that is only because I can't get certain things on vinyl. CD's are also easier to carry. However, I prefer to work with vinyl because the sound is better than digital. You just can't beat the sound (or smell) of virgin vinyl played on a moving coil cartridge with analogue pre-amps and power amps through some serious speakers properly placed in an acoustically friendly room. Period.

Any difficult DJing situations?
I was working at a club in New York City and the promoter was a Swedish bloke who had a real prejudice against hip-hop and told me I couldn't play it. One night I show up to work to find the club has been booked for a private party for New York's basketball team The Knicks. And I had no hip-hop. And these guys still towered over me even though the DJ booth was raised. Luckily I had enough funk classics to somewhat pull it off but it was tricky. A word of advice: never listen to promoters who tell you what they think you should play. Trust your own instincts and bring a wide variety.

Advice for an aspiring DJ?

The mixing part is easy. I seriously think you could teach a monkey to mix (and it would be a damn fun experiment). DJing all starts with programming so concentrate more on why certain records work together whether it's sonically, thematically, or stylistically. And work on your record collection.

Advice to aspiring female DJs?

If you are serious about music and DJing, do not use your gender to get work. Just work on your craft and remember that in any profession, a woman always has to work harder than her male counterpart to be taken seriously.

Yousef

DJ style: House

Can be heard at: Creamfields or Circus, Liverpool

What's the best thing about DJing?

It's my job. Really that as good as it gets. I love DJing and rocking a party but being able to earn a living doing something I really enjoy is happiness.

Useful mixing tip?

If you can't beat match on Technics try and understand that the numbers on the pitch are percentages and you can usually get the beats in time if one deck is exactly on point and the other deck is exactly on another.

Do you mix with MP3s? How does it compare to vinyl and CDs?

I will always love the sound of vinyl overall; MP3s are naturally brighter sounding which is good though.

Do you use Final Scratch or Ableton Live? What do you think of this new technology?

I've never used either but I will be getting into Ableton this year. I'm quite a creative DJ so this will be good for me.

What advice would you give an aspiring DJ?

Get stuck in. Don't be afraid. The job, although tough and lonely sometimes, is worth it. Trust me.

Chris Duckenfield

DJ style: House, techno, disco

Can be heard at: Scuba, Sheffield; Fabric, London

How do you see DJing?
The responsibility to entertain and hopefully enlighten in equal measure. Having to provide the soundtrack to people's weekend release is not something to be taken lightly! The travel, food and friend-making perks are not be sniffed at either.

Two useful mixing tips?
1 Know your tracks, blending at appropriate points in the tune makes things much easier.
2 Don't be afraid to use small sections of records as breaks or bridges, no one ever said you had to play tracks end to end.

Do you mix with MP3s? How does it compare to vinyl and CDs?
Yes, but the sound quality does vary wildly, although unfortunately, being as most clubs tend not to prioritise the sound system, it's generally not a problem. CDs tend to be much punchier and 'drier' sounding than vinyl, so keep your eyes (and ears) on the mixer when using multiple formats.

Do you use Final Scratch or Ableton Live? What do you think of this new technology?
We [his production outfit Swag] use Ableton in our 'Decks And Gadgets' shows, going from laptop to CD/turntable is great fun and very versatile.

What is the future for DJing?
I'd like to think some of the younger DJs coming through will return to, or at least incorporate, a more varied style of DJing. One-dimensional sets have always been dull. New technologies can only increase that diversity and forward thinking musical spirit.

What's the worse disaster that has happened to you whilst DJing?
The old 'taking the wrong record/CD off' classic is always a favourite. To be honest most equipment-related adversity (i.e. one deck) can bring out the best in you. Pilot error however (especially substance related), is usually less easy to cope with.

What advice would you give an aspiring DJ?
Get a trade, just in case. Do you how few plumbers there are in the world? No really, it's a cliché, but it still rings true – do your

own thing, don't be afraid to take risks and most importantly, don't be mediocre or support mediocre music.

What was your big break into DJing?
Friends of mine asked a local club with a lacklustre Friday night if we could have a chance to turn the night around. I had plenty of records, but had never touched a pair of decks in my life. I learned the craft there, the night became very popular and that was the beginning of everything, really.

Sandy Rivera, Kings of Tomorrow

DJ style: Soulful house

Can be heard at: Ministry of Sound; Pacha, London

What's the best thing about DJing?
Watching people let loose on the dancefloor.

Two useful mixing tips?
Stay on time with the mix, and know your records inside out.

Preferred format?
I prefer CDs at this point. I put my vinyl on CD to play out.

What advice would you give an aspiring DJ?
Don't conform to politics in this industry. And if you are a good DJ, get into producing, the two go hand in hand these days.

Rob da Bank

DJ style: Eclectic: chill-out to reggae to hip-hop to Dolly Parton

Can be heard at: Sunday Best; Bestival; BBC Radio 1

What do you love about DJing?
Going to crazy beach parties in Poland; DJing up mountains in Argentina; or just playing a local pub in London with your mates gets 10/10 every time!

Two useful mixing tips?
1 I'm definitely not a technical DJ so I'd have to say worry more about what the crowd looks like rather than what's gonna seamlessly mix in next.
2 Keep 'em guessing. I never stick with one style all night. If that's what you do cool but don't be scared to experiment; the worse that can happen is you never DJ again and lose all your friends ... hmm.

Do you mix with MP3s?

I'm not proud of it but I've never downloaded an MP3 let alone DJed with one, but my miniature brain is gradually being dragged into the 21st century and I totally see the point. I think most (sane) DJs can now see that vinyl will always exist in our lifetimes so all the other tools are just bonus bits.

Do you use Final Scratch or Ableton Live?

Umm, again you're talking to the wrong DJ. I did do my Fabric mix CD on Ableton Live because it gets everything perfect but I don't wanna be perfect when I DJ in a club. My mistakes are some of favourite moments when I DJ!

What is the future for DJing?

Bring on the kids and kick us old duffers off the decks!

Any funny DJing stories?

My record got stuck twice on New Year's Eve – the crowd were laughing with me so I span it back, ripped it off the decks and threw it into the crowd. Two days later I got an email saying I'd nearly knocked someone's girlfriend out and they'd all had to leave and I was a git. Fair enough!

Advice for aspiring DJs?

I really believe it's a lot to do with luck. That's not very encouraging but I've heard so many DJs who are miles better than most big DJs and they never get the breaks. Obviously you need to stick at it, definitely start your own night and try and be different. I never even wanted to be a 'proper' DJ; it just happened that way but it was ten years of playing before I could make a living off it.

Do you see any problems with DJ culture at the moment?

No, never have done. My cup is always half full and the periodic doom-smiths who say it's all over or complain that there's too much trance or too many DJs playing Venezuelan bhangra trance are just boring. It's never been better!

Advice on radio DJing?

It's about having your own style. I had no radio experience at all when I started at Radio 1 (although I think it could be useful if you want to do daytime or commercial radio). Your taste and knowledge of music is much more important than knowing how to wire up a microphone or having a wonderful voice. I mean, look at me!

10

when it all goes wrong, when it all goes right

In this chapter you will learn:
• about some of the hiccups and joy you may experience on the way to being a successful DJ.

Ask any DJ about nights where it has gone wrong for them and they are likely to tell you countless tales of DJing disasters. Lots can go wrong after all. The equipment can fail, the records can jump, the crowd might not turn up, the promoter might not pay you or, worse still, people just might not dance.

I've had my fair share of disasters. For instance, I was booked to do the midnight slot on New Year's Eve at The End the year the club opened. I was thrilled to be playing such a great venue with a lovely, well-thought out sound system. I had been given some great test pressings of unreleased tracks by various artists who were perfect for The End's crowd, including music by Basement Jaxx that no one had yet heard.

Intending to mix new tracks with underground classics, after a countdown to midnight, 'bang' – I was off with a forgotten gem that had everybody dancing. I cue-ed up the Basement Jaxx track and was halfway through blending it in when 'crash!' – all the music stopped, the house lights came up and 600 or so previously smiling people turned round and looked at me with death threats in their eyes. It was a disaster. The fire alarm had been tripped within the venue and all the sound went off and the lights went up. It was nothing to do with me but the crowd didn't know that and for about a minute, which is a lifetime in terms of the dancefloor, I was mortified and able to do nothing. Fortunately, once I was back in control of the sound everything went smoothly, but it certainly wasn't a gig to forget.

There is an expression 'Worse things happen at sea'. And it's true. Another DJ and myself were asked to play for two days on a ferry going from Harwich to Hamburg. Young clubbers were enticed to part with a large sum of money to dance on board to the latest club sounds before retiring to their cabins and waking up in the coastal port in north Germany. With an itinerary that planned yet more dancing for the return trip, it seemed like a novel and fun idea on paper and what's more the money was good.

Bringing a wide variety of tunes I thought I had every eventuality covered. Except the weather that is. We arrived in Harwich to a full storm, with dark clouds unleashing a torrent into a sea of colossal waves. At this point the conditions were officially gale force seven. It didn't seem to daunt the captain though, who was no doubt at ease wading through the North Sea in his particularly huge Scandinavian ferry which was clearly built to withstand such circumstances. The same cannot be said for Technics decks. They are mighty machines that will rarely let you down, but by the time we had set them up, we were in the full throws of a highly impressive gale force nine North Sea storm.

In what was deemed an entertainment lounge with 300 or so pleasure seekers all waiting for the first tune, we were getting a little worried. Not only would the needle instantly fly off the record, but the solitary non-DJ friendly CD player would jump making it hard to even play the few CDs we had brought. To boot, everything that wasn't nailed down was falling from one side of the room to the other including the dancers who at this point more resembled acrobats cart-wheeling from one wall to another.

Add to this a free-flowing bar, sea sickness, endless amounts of travel sickness tablets distributed by the crew, and we had what amounted to a farce on our hands. Yet with the aid of two duvets placed under each deck and about twenty pounds worth of coins stuck on top of each needle, we were finally able to perform a strange new type of DJing. As we slid around at the mercy of the ferocious sea, we probably hit upon numerous new forms of scratching moves that night, as the crowd veered across the dancefloor occasionally in time to the erratic beats.

Truly a DJing disaster at sea then. But I wouldn't have missed it for all the life jackets in China. My point is, things can go wrong when DJing, and they will. But for all the mishaps and embarrassing silences, there are the unforgettable moments when it all goes right and you and the crowd are at one with the music. The feeling of playing a new piece of music that you are really excited about to a crowd who gets it, is priceless. You are getting the chance to share a wonderful art form with people and watch them respond to it. To think that you are actually getting paid to play the music you love is incredible.

DJing regularly is hard work but it is worth it. I've been lucky enough to play amazing festivals and great clubs in the UK and abroad. Some of the best DJing experiences I've had have been on state-of-the-art sound systems but also in friends' houses, bars and even pubs. Sharing music is a real pleasure; if you've got the bug, you'll do it anywhere.

Try to get a residency somewhere. This is perhaps the best way to become a master of DJing. Resident DJs give nights their individual flavour and identity, but what's more, a residency gives you unprecedented access to a regular crowd. It gives you the chance to really learn what music and mixing tricks work best. Strive to get a residency and build a rapport with your audience. Learn from them about what they love, and teach them how to have even more fun by stretching the crazy sounds and music you give them.

DJing should be adventurous and exhilarating. It's your job as a budding DJ to push for this. Do not conform to being a DJ robot. We have jukeboxes and iPods for that. Challenge your listeners to enjoy themselves more. It's great to see what you can get away with.

The new arsenal of technology at your disposal puts even more opportunity to be daring and intrepid into your hands. Since writing this, technology will have continued to march on. The digital age means technology moves incredibly fast and new machines, software and gadgets are available in the high street all the time. Keeping up is no mean feat. Keeping on top of it means you will be at the cutting edge of what DJs are able to do. Even ten years ago DJs would be amazed at what they can now do. However, remember that despite all the technology and gadgets on the market, DJing is still essentially about expressing a passion for music in a creative and entertaining way. Technology can't do this for you; it must come from within.

As more studio production techniques come within their grasp, DJs have the ability to be far more creative. Whereas the Technics 1200 turntables are likely to always be the icon of DJ and club culture, it is software programmes like Traktor and Ableton Live that make the future of DJing so exciting. Mastering the science of manipulating records and DJ tricks is one thing; live remixing and blending non-dance music is another. Instead of just manipulating the physical format of music, if you are comfortable using software, you can alter the very music itself. If you are willing to learn this 'musician-led' form of DJing by adopting live remixing, you have a very good chance of making a name for yourself by playing very unique sets. Your passion for DJing could then turn you into a musician.

If you are prepared to dedicate your life to the passion you have for music, you have got what it takes to be a good DJ. It is a lifetime commitment too. Keep at it and you will get better and better. Watch other DJs. Befriend other DJs. Concentrate on finding good music as well as tracks that no one else has. Don't restrict yourself to one style. There is a whole universe of mind-blowing music to discover. It's your job to explore this universe rather than play what Pete Tong, Judge Jules or Tim Westwood is playing. Purchase old music as well as new and study the history of it. Doing this will make you a better DJ. You must be dedicated and be yourself. If you can do that, you are ready to share the music and you should have plenty of amazing nights ahead of you.

Like records, though, DJing is full of lows as well as highs. Established working DJs, DJs just starting to get their first bookings, and even big-name DJs who travel the world from one cherry-picked gig to another all have bad nights and good nights. It just happens like that.

However, when a set goes really well, you can experience one of the best feelings in the world. Hundreds of smiling people jumping up and down with their arms in the air enjoying every second of the music you are spinning. There is only one thing better. And that's the next track. You know what the next track is and you can instinctively feel that they are going to adore it too. This is the moment you are at one with the crowd, together in music. This is when you, and all the people around you, are lost in music.

Now go share those tunes.

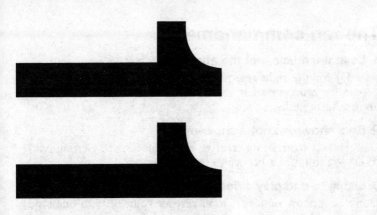

11

the ten commandments

In this chapter you will learn:
- the ten golden rules of
  performing as a DJ.

The ten commandments

1 Love the music, not the attention

Be a DJ for the right reason. Be passionate about entertaining people by bringing great music to their ears and feet. It's all about sharing music.

2 Be a showman not a show-off

Gain respect from being creative and professional. Getting paid to DJ is a job, not a licence to be an idiot.

3 Listen to and play different kinds of music

Don't be narrow-minded. Don't restrict yourself with one type of music. There are so many great records out there, old and new. Funky house is not enough. Concentrate on finding and playing only one type of music: good music.

4 Be original, use the element of surprise, take risks

Music should be exciting not bland. Use the fantastic opportunities that digital technology gives you to remix and loop tracks. Don't be dictated to by fashion and above all be yourself.

5 Think about what the dancefloor wants

... and not about that new Kompakt or Definitive Juxx white label that you are dying to hear on a big sound system. Learn to read the dancefloor and be responsive.

6 Structure your set

Have a beginning, middle and end with ups and downs and mind-blowing surprises. Always leave them wanting more.

7 Use the equipment correctly

Respect people's ears, don't bang it out; distorted music sounds rubbish. Watch your levels.

8 Don't overuse tricks

Let the music speak – don't cram a set with endless tricks, use them with stealth ... unless you are a scratch DJ, in which case perform like a man possessed who happens to have five arms.

9 Be friendly and polite, have fun

Follow the rules of DJ etiquette and don't forget to have fun. You are getting paid to have a great time. It's incredible!

10 Don't eye up the bouncer's girlfriend

It's dangerous to your health.

12

taking it further

Books

Adventures On The Wheels Of Steel by Dave Haslam (Fourth Estate, 2001)
Somewhat inconsistent accounts of various superstar DJs and their exploits

Altered State by Matthew Collin (Serpent's Tail, 1997)
Excellent social history of acid house culture

Energy Flash: Journey Through Rave Music And Dance Culture by Simon Reynolds (Picador, 1998)
A look at the explosion of dance music at the end of the '80s

How To DJ Right by Frank Broughton and Bill Brewster (Grove Press, 2003)
Extensive study of the science of DJing

Last Night A DJ Saved My Life by Bill Brewster and Frank Broughton (Headline, 2000)
Broad and comprehensive history of DJ culture

Love Saves The Day by Tim Lawrence (Duke University Press, 2004)
In-depth and absorbing history of US dance music in the '70s

Music Industry Manual: DJ, Nightclub, Promoter Handbook by James Robertson (Music Industry Manual, 2004)
Directory of useful contacts and information

Music Week Directory by Nick Tesco (CMP Information, 2004)
Extensive list of music business contact details

Pump Up the Volume by Sean Bidder (Channel 4, 2001)
Fun history of acid house

The Rough Guide To Drum'n'Bass by Peter Shapiro (Rough Guide, 1999)
A–Z of drum'n'bass music

The Rough Guide To Hip-Hop by Peter Shapiro (Rough Guide, 2005)
A–Z of hip-hop music

The Rough Guide To House by Sean Bidder (Rough Guide, 1999)
A–Z of house music

The Rough Guide To Reggae by Steve Barrow and Peter Dalton (Rough Guide, 2004)
Info on building a good reggae and ragga collection

The Rough Guide To Soul Music by Peter Shapiro (Rough Guide, 2000)
Info on building a good soul music collection

The Rough Guide To Techno by Tim Barr (Rough Guide, 2000)
A–Z of techno music

The Guerrila Guide To The Music Business by Sarah Davis and Dave Laing (Continuum, 2001)
Deals with every aspect of making and selling music

The Mobile DJ Handbook by Stacy Zemon (Focal Press, 2003)
How to build a successful career as a mobile DJ

Videos/DVDs

DJ's Complete Guide
Step-by-step instructions on learning to DJ

So you Want to be a DJ
Insider tips

The Art of Turntablism
Scratch techniques

Magazines

Big Shot
US dance and electronic scene

Clash
Indie and dance music interviews and reviews

DJ Mag
Dance music interviews, reviews and equipment profiles

FACT
Fun, vinyl-loving 7"-shaped magazine for dance music enthusiasts

Hip-Hop Connection
All aspects of UK/US hip-hop scene

IDJ
Dance music interviews, reviews and equipment profiles

Knowledge
Drum'n'bass and its scene with interviews, reviews and listings

M8
Scottish dance music title with interviews and reviews

Mixmag
Clubbing lifestyle title with interviews, reviews and listings

Music Week
Music industry trade magazine

The Source
US hip-hop and R'n'B

Touch
R'n'B, hip-hop and urban music and club culture

Vibe
US dance music and hip-hop

Update
Weekly roundup of new dance music releases

XL8R
US electronic music scene with interviews and reviews

DJ and music-based websites

All Music – http://www.allmusic.com
Fairly comprehensive, well-written biographies and discographies
on thousands of recording artists

Battle Sounds – http://www.battlesounds.com
Q-bert shows scratching styles

B-boy – http://www.b-boy.com
US-based hip-hop site

Deep House Network – http://www.deephousenetwork.com
Deep house fan site

Digital Scratch – http://www.digitalscratch.com
A site on scratching CDs and MP3s

DMC – http://www.dmcworld.com

International DJ competitions, publisher and record label

Drum'n'bass Arena – http://www.breakbeat.co.uk
Drum'n'bass fan site

Fat Lace – http://www.fatlacemagazine.com
Online magazine for 'ageing B-Boys'

Sphere of Hip-Hop – http://www.sphereofhiphop.com
Hip-hop reviews, interviews and resources

Thud Rumble – http://www.thudrumble.com
Scratch DJ community

Trust the DJ – http://www.trusttheDJ.com
Large online DJ community and shop

UK Music Jobs – http://www.uk.music-jobs.com
Online bulletin board for jobs in the music industry

Online download shops

All these recommended stores sell MP3s which have no DRM
(digital rights management) restrictions, although some may sell
watermarked downloads. Make sure you check what you are
buying and look for high bit rate files.

Bleep – http://www.bleep.com
Legal electronic music download store (MP3)

ClickGroove – http://www.clickgroove.com
Legal soulful dance music download store (MP3)

DJ Download – http://www.djdownload.com
DJ Magazine's legal dance music download store (MP3)

KarmaDownload – http://www.karmadownload.com
Legal download store specialising in independent labels (MP3)

Trax Source – http://www.traxsource.com
Legal house music downloads with lots of labels

TuneTribe – http://www.tunetribe.com
Easy-to-use legal music download store specialising in cutting-
edge independent label music (MP3) and cherry-picked major
label back catalogue (WMA) alongside music articles

Record shops selling CDs and vinyl online

A1 Record Finders – http://www.aonerecordfinders.com
Massive vinyl only store

Crazy Beat – http://www.crazybeat.co.uk/
Black music record shop with extensive back catalogue specialising in soul, disco, house and rap

DJ Friendly – http://www.djfriendly.co.uk/
Great online record shop specialising in rare gems, particularly good for disco and old-school rap

eBay – http://www.ebay.com
You know this one!

GEMM – http://www.gemm.com
Site which searches record shops around the world

Global Groove – http://www.globalgroove.co.uk
Dance music store

Hard to Find Records – http://www.htfr.co.uk
Online record and DJ equipment store

Juno – http://www.juno.co.uk
Online dance music store

Net Sounds – http://www.netsoundsmusic.com
Amazing music market place – great for finding pretty much anything

Phonica – http://www.phonicarecords.co.uk
Superb online record store great for upfront electro, house, techno, leftfield, reggae and disco

Pure Pleasure Music – http://www.purepleasuremusic.com
Dance music including jazz, Latin, disco and hip-hop

Reckless – http://www.reckless.co.uk
Well-known London second-hand record and CD shop

Scenario – http://www.scenariorecords.com
Respected London shop selling hip-hop, soul, R'n'B, battle weapons, reggae

Vinyl Exchange – http://www.vinylexchnage.co.uk
Well-known Manchester-based second-hand record and CD shop

Vinyl Junkies – http://www.vinyl-junkies.co.uk
Shop and online store dealing in deep, funky, jazzy, soulful house and disco

Worldwide Record Stores – http://www.moremusic.co.uk
Second-hand records and CDs

Record shops

Recommended record shops that have good dance, electronic, soul, drum'n'bass, reggae or hip-hop music catalogue

National

Fopp – http://www.fopp.co.uk
HMV – http://www.hmv.co.uk
Virgin Megastore – http://www.virginmegastores.co.uk

Birmingham

Hard to Find – http://www.htfr.com
Massive – http://www.massiverecords.com

Brighton

Rounder Records

Edinburgh

Underground Solushn

Glasgow

Carbon
Rubadub – http://www.rubadub.co.uk
23rd Precinct – http://www.23rdprecinct.co.uk

Leeds

Crash – http://www.crashrecords.co.uk

Leicester

2 Funky

Liverpool

3 Beat – http://www.3beatrecords.co.uk

London

Blackmarket – http://www.blackmarket.co.uk
Disque – http://www.disque.co.uk
Honest Jon's – http://www.honestjons.com
Phonica – http://www.phonicarecords.co.uk
Pure Groove – http://www.puregroove.co.uk
Reckless Records – http://www.reckless.co.uk
Rough Trade – http://www.roughtrade.com
Scenario – http://www.scenariorecords.com
Selectadisc – http://www.selectadisc.co.uk
Sister Ray – http://www.sisterray.co.uk
Smallfish – http://www.smallfish.co.uk
Soul and Dance Exchange
Sounds of the Universe – http://www.souljazzrecords.co.uk
Uptown – http://www.uptownrecords.com
Vinyl Junkies – http://www.vinyl-junkies.co.uk

Manchester

Eastern Bloc – http://www.easternblocrecords.co.uk
Fat City – http://www.fatcity.co.uk
Piccadilly Records – http://www.piccadillyrecords.com
Vox Pop – http://www.voxpoprecords.com

Nottingham

Funky Monkey – http://www.funkymonkey.co.uk
Selectadisc – http://www.selectadisc.co.uk

Oxford

Massive – http://www.massiverecords.com

Selby

Tune Inn – http://www.tuneinn.com

Upminister

Crazy Beat – http://www.crazybeat.co.uk

DJ equipment and software manufacturers

Ableton – http://www.ableton.com
Allen & Heath – http://www.allen-heath.co.uk
Citronic – http://www.citronic.com
Demon – http://www.del.demon.com
Gemini – http://www.geminidj.com
Korg – http://www.korg.co.uk
Native Instruments – http://www.nativeinstruments.de
Numark – http://www.numark.com
Pioneer – http://www.pioneer.co.uk
Sennheiser – http://www.sennheiser.com
Sony – http://www.sony.co.uk
Stanton – http://www.stantondj.com/v2/index
Technics – http://www.technics1210.com
Vestax – http://www.vestax.co.uk

DJ equipment shops and online stores

Disco Studio – http://www.discostudio.co.uk
DJ Needs – http://www.djneeds.com
DJ Superstore – http://www.djsuperstore.co.uk
Guildford Sound and Light – http://www.guildfordsoundandlight.
  com
Hard to Find Records – http://www.htfr.com
Maidstone Disco Supplies – http://www.discosupplies.net
Richer Sounds – http://www.richersounds.com

Sapphires – http://www.sapphires.co.uk
Studiospares – http://www.studiospares.com
The DJ Shop – http://www.prodjsupplies.co.uk
Turn Key – http://www.turnkey.uk.com
Youngs Disco Centre – http://www.youngsdisco.com

Organisations and courses

Academy of Contemporary Music – http://www.acm.ac.uk
DJ courses run in association with Vestax

DJ Academy Organisation – http://www.djacademy.otg.uk
One-day, ten-week DJ and radio presenting courses based in
Worcester

DMC Ltd – http://www.dmcworld.com
International DJ organisation which runs mixing championships

International Turntablist Federation – http://www.hip-hop.com
US-, Europe- and Japan-based hip-hop organisation

Point Blank – http://www.point-blank.co.uk
Courses tailor made for budding DJs

Red Bull DJ Academy – http://www.redbullmusicacademy.com
Large annual international gathering of DJ teachers and pupils

Sub Bass DJ and Music Production School – http://www.
subbassdj.com)
Professional, DJ-run courses with no more than four pupils per
course

Technics DJ Academy – http://www.dj-academy.com
Manchester-based, short, one-to-one and career courses for
beginners to experts

Club promo mailing lists

All these promotion companies will have tough criteria for
getting on to their mailing lists. You will need to prove you are
regularly DJing or hosting a radio show to get on their books.

Hyperactive – http://www.music-house.co.uk/hyperactive
Funky house, tech house, progressive house, trance, urban

Power Promotions – http://www.power.co.uk
Across the board from commercial and underground dance to pop music

Rocket Science – http://www.rocketsciencemedia.com
Underground house, techno and leftfield music

Rude Awakening
Underground deep, jazzy, vocal house

Sony BMG Urban – http://www.so-urban.co.uk
R'n'B, urban, hip-hop

Waxworks – http://www.music-house.co.uk/waxworks
Breakbeat, electronica, drum'n'bass and hip-hop promotion

White Noise – http://www.whitenoisepromo.com
Cutting-edge electronica, house, techno and beats. Run through a subscription service which sends promo music in return for a monthly fee.

Zzonked – http://www.zzonked.co.uk
Hip-hop, leftfield, downtempo, breaks and beats

Further information for radio DJs

BBC – http://www.bbc.co.uk/newtalent
The BBC's radio trainee schemes and jobs page

Broadcast
Weekly trade magazine

OFCOM – http://www.ofcom.org.uk/radio
Regulatory body that polices the airwaves

Radio Now – http://www.radio-now.co.uk
Directory of UK stations and webcasts

The Guardian Media Section
Job ads and articles about the industry, on Mondays in the newspaper or online at http://media.guardian.co.uk/

DJ events, conferences and festivals

Key dance music, hip-hop and industry events in the calendar include:

- MIDEM (January – Cannes)
- Winter Music Conference (WMC) (March – Miami)
- Homelands (May – Winchester)
- Ibiza club season (June–Sept – Ibiza)
- Sonar (June – Barcelona)
- Glastonbury (June – Pilton)
- Global Gathering (July – Stratford-Upon-Avon)
- The Big Chill (August – Herefordshire)
- TDK Cross Central (August – London)
- Creamfields (August – Liverpool)
- Bestival (September – Isle of Wight)
- In the City (September – Manchester)
- DMC Championship (September – Worldwide)
- Amsterdam Dance Event (October – Amsterdam)

glossary

A capella A vocal without instrumental accompaniment.
Acetate Or 'dub plate'. A test pressing on soft vinyl that has a limited lifespan as it can only be played a few times.

Analogue Sound processed in the non-digital way.

Antiskating Device on a turntable to correct the pull of the needle to the centre of the record.

Baby scratch Basic one-handed scratch.

Back-to-back mixing Mixing technique using two copies of the same tune allowing the DJ to add in beats to create an echo effect. Also a term used by DJs who wish to DJ together by playing one record each after one another.

Bar A small unit of music which is usually four beats long in dance music.

Beat The constant pulse of a particular rhythm.

Beat counter Device that measures the tempo of a tune in BPM.

Beat juggle Technique of using individual drum beats or two sections of two tunes to create a new rhythm or loop.

Beat match Technique of adjusting the speeds of two separate tunes to syncopate their beats.

Beat mixing Technique of mixing two tunes together so that the beats and phrases are syncopated together.

Bit rate A bit rate is the amount of information (or bits) that is transferred per second (bit per second or bps). MP3s are measured in thousands of bits per second (kbps) and the higher the kbps, the higher the sound quality.

Blend A smooth transition from one record to another.

Bootleg A record that is illegal as it has been made using musical material without the permission of the copyright holder.

BPM Beats per minute – the measurement of the tempo or speed of a track.

Break Part of a track where the music drops down to just a rhythm and percussion section.

Breakbeat Originates from early hip-hop where DJs would loop up the breaks from different songs or funk records. These looped-together drum parts became known as breakbeats. Now it is also used to describe a sub-genre of dance music that uses breakbeat rhythms.

Breakdown Part of a track where the rhythm section is taken out leaving only the musical or vocal elements.

Cans Slang for headphones.

Cartridge Holds the stylus on the end of the tone arm and converts the vibrations of the needle into electronic signals.

Channel An individual sound signal. Different mixers have different numbers of channels depending on how many things it can mix together.

Crossfader The control on the mixer that allows you to fade from one channel to another.

Copyright The legal ownership of a piece of music.

Counterweight Or tone arm weight. The weight on the opposite end of the tone arm to the needle that counteracts the force or 'torque' of the needle bearing down on the grooves of a record.

Cue Listening to the next record in your headphones, or finding the right starting place of the next record.

Cut Fast switch from one track to another without losing a beat. Sometimes referred to as 'drop mixing'.

Decks Turntables or CD players.

Delay A sound effect used to make timed echoes of selected elements in a track.

Digital The way sound is recorded on certain formats such as MP3, DAT, CD or Minidisc. The sound is saved in groups of ones and zeros.

Distortion A loud dirty sound that happens when a sound signal goes through equipment at too high a volume thus distorting it. Some sound effects boxes allow you to add this as an effect.

Download The act of taking a file from a website and loading it on to a computer. Therefore, in terms of downloading music, this means putting a music file such as an MP3 on to your computer.

Drop mixing Technique used to fade from one tune to another without losing a beat.

Dub Originates from Jamaica where a dub is a stripped-down remix of a reggae tune. In dance music it is also used to refer to a basic version of a tune where the vocals have been reduced.

Dubplate See 'acetate'.

Echo A sound effect that repeats sounds.

EQ Or equalisation. Adjustment of separate frequencies such as bass, mid-range or treble.

Fade Gradual adjustment of volume or sound levels between one channel and another.

Feedback Horrible screechy sound caused by electrical equipment picking up its own signals.

Filtering A sound effect which blocks certain frequencies.

Flanging A sound effect used to add whooshing noises.

Flare A type of scratch where the fader is used as an off switch.

Four/four Music which has a time signature of four beats to the bar.

FX Or effects. Electronic boxes allowing the DJ to create effects. These play with the sound in particular ways such as adding delay, echo or phasing.

Gain Control on a mixer which allows you to add volume to a channel, e.g. so you can turn up a quiet track.

Gating Effect used to cut a track up to produce a rhythmic staccato sound.

Groove Either the spiral trench of a record that the needle sits in or repetitive pattern of drums and bass line in a track that people dance to.

Head shell Piece at the end of the tone arm that connects the cartridge to the tone arm.

Hook The infectious part of a track that people remember.

KBPS Kilobits per second. MP3s are measured in thousands of bits per second (kbps) and the higher the kbps, the higher the sound quality.

Key A group of notes that work together in harmony.

Kick drum The bass drum which drives dance music.

Kill switch Control on the mixer which allows the DJ to instantly kill the bass, mid-range or treble frequencies.

Line-in/phono switch Input selector for a channel on a mixer.

Loop A repeated part of a track.

Mailing list List of DJs who get sent promo records.

MC Mic-controller. Person who uses the microphone to sing, rap or speak over music.

Melody Part of the track that sits on top of the drums and bass line played, for example, on the piano, guitar or horns.

Mid-range The frequencies between the treble and bass.

Mixer Machine that lets you merge sound signals from different sources.

Mixing Act of joining different pieces of music together.

Monitors Speakers near the DJ booth which give the DJ a clear sound of what is happening on the dancefloor.

MP3 A common type of compressed digital audio file.

PA Usually refers to the sound system (as in public address system) but can mean a live act (as in public appearance).

Percussion Drums and other instruments such as bongos which create the rhythm of a track.

Phasing Whooshing effect caused by two parts of the same record being played at the same time with a slight delay.

Phono From 'phonograph' meaning turntable but used to indicate the inputs for turntables on a mixer.

Phrase Block of a track's structure which is four bars long.

Pirate radio Radio station that doesn't have a legal licence to operate.

Pitch Used to refer to how high a note is or how fast a record is.

Pitch control Controller on a DJ turntable or CD deck used to adjust a track's tempo.

Pitch bend Control used to fractionally speed up or slow down a track so it can match another.

Platter The round part of a turntable that the record sits on.

Programming The way in which a DJ structures a set in terms of what tunes are played and in what order.

Promo 'Promotional' records or CDs given away to help publicise a track before it is released.

Promoter Person who organises club nights and books the DJs.

Re-edit A new version of a track made by cutting up different sections of the original and re-arranging them.

Remix A new version of a track made by reorganising parts of the original's musical elements and possibly adding new ones.

Residency A regular booking at the same venue, could be weekly or monthly making him or her a 'resident' DJ.

Reverb A sound effect that adds the ambience of a room to the mix.

Rhythm A pattern of sound created by a track's percussion.

Rub A scratch technique where a hand is kept on a record to slow it down.

Sampling Act of taking part of a record and using it in another.

Scratching A technique used for rhythmically manipulating a record back and forth whilst using the fader on a mixer to chop up the rhythm.

Sequencer Computer programme which records music as a series of instructions for other instruments to follow.

Selector A DJ.

Set The entire music and length of time a DJ plays during a performance.

Slipmat Felt mat that sits between the record and platter to allow a DJ to hold the record without stopping the turntable.

Snare drum The drum with a loud 'thwack' sound.

Spinback Technique using one hand to quickly spin a record back to create a rewind sound.

Split-cue Control on the mixer which allows you to hear one track in each ear of your headphones.

Stab Scratch technique like a cut but faster so a high-pitched scratch sound is produced.

Stylus The needle that sits in the grooves of a record.

Tear Scratch technique that, by halting a record, creates a minute gap in the sound.

Tempo The speed of a track.

Test pressing Early run-offs of a record before it is mass manufactured done to test the sound quality of the music. These are often given away to DJs to promote the record.

Tone arm The arm on a turntable that holds the cartridge.

Tone arm weight Or counterbalance. The weight on the opposite end of the tone arm to the needle that counteracts the force or 'torque' of the needle bearing down on the grooves of a record.

Transform Scratch technique where the crossfader or line-in/phono switch is used like an on-switch whilst chopping up a scratch into little rhythmic pieces.

Turntables Record players or decks.

Turntablism The art of using turntables as musical instruments through scratching and other techniques.

Tweeter A treble speaker.

Warp marker Indicate where a track's beats are within a digital audio file.

White label A record distributed without a record company so that the label is blank.

Woofer A bass speaker.

appendix 1

Turntable features

Turntable features	What it does
Adapter	Secures 7" singles to the spindle if they have large holes.
Anti-skate control	Keeps the needle in the groove.
Cartridge	Turns the vibrations from the needle into electronic signals.
Counterweight	Stops the needle being too heavy on the record by balancing the weight of the cartridge.
Cueing lever	Lifts the front of the tone arm off or on the record.
Earth lead	Connects with the screw on the back of the mixer to prevent annoying humming sounds.
Headshell	Piece at the end of the tone arm that connects the cartridge to the tone arm.
Height-adjust stick	Raises or lowers the complete tone arm.
Light	Lights up the grooves on the record allowing the DJ to see how far through the track the needle is. On Technics these bulbs usually fail after three to four years giving you an indication how old the deck is if it's second-hand.

Phono leads	Take the sound from the deck to the mixer.
Pitch control	Slide control that allows you to match records with different tempos by speeding up or slowing down the rotation of the platter. Technics have a +/–8 per cent range whilst others may have +/–16 per cent or even +/–30 per cent.
Platter	The round plate that spins.
Power switch	Turns the machine on and off.
Speed button	Moves the speed to either 33 rpm or 45 rpm.
Spindle	The metal rod in the middle of the platter.
Start/stop button	Hit it once to get the platter spinning. Hit it again to stop.
Strobe light	A flashing light that doesn't need to be used by DJs but is there to indicate how close to 33rpm or 45rpm the platter is spinning. The dots on the side of the platter stand still when perfectly on 33rpm or 45rpm.
Stylus	The needle that sits in the record's grooves.
Tone arm	The arm that carries the needle, skating across the record.

CD deck features

CD deck feature	What it does
Cue	This sets a cue point when the track is paused, and takes you straight back to that point when the track is playing.
Data memory	Using a memory card you can save cue points so that they are there next time you play that track.
Hot cue	Enables you to go back to marked cue points when the track is playing.
Jog wheel (sometimes this might be a joystick)	Allows you to cue up a track by moving slowly through the music to find the point you want to start from. You can also use it to adjust the pitch when the track is playing.
Loop controls	Allows you to loop up sections of music through a built-in sampler.
Master tempo	Allows you to adjust a track's tempo without altering the pitch. Very handy!
Play/pause	Start/stop button
Power switch	On/off
Read-out	Displays the track number and counter which shows the time remaining. Can also display the track's tempo in beats per minute.
Reverse	Play tracks backwards.

Search	Fast forwards within a track.
Tempo control adjust	Changes the range of tempo control, e.g. from +/–8 per cent to +/–16 per cent.
Tempo/pitch control	Alters the speed of the track so you can match different tempos.
Track search	Allows you to skip to particular tracks.
Vinyl emulation	Enables you to use the CD deck's platter to control the CD as if it was vinyl.

Mixer features

Mixer features	What it does
Booth output	Controls the volume of the monitor speaker.
Channel fader	Each channel represents one source of music. A typical mixer might have two channels (one for each turntable for instance) whilst another might have three or four (so that you use CD decks as well as turntables).
Cueing switches/buttons	Enable you to listen to each channel separately from the music playing.
Crossfader	Moves across from one channel to another, fading each channel's music in and out. This allows you to blend or cut between tracks.
Crossfader curve control	Changes the degree of volume when moving the crossfader across.
FX	More expensive mixers often have built-in FX (effects) for changing the signal with, e.g. reverb, echo or filters.
FX send/return	Lets you use an external FXs unit.
Gains/trim	Boosts the volume of each channel fractionally, allowing you to turn up quiet records.

Hamster switch/ crossfader assign	Chooses which two channels the crossfade fades between. Turntablists make good use of this.
Headphone volume	Allows you to adjust the volume of your headphones.
Kill switches	Turn off different bands of the EQ, i.e. the bass or middle or treble.
Level indicators	A display of green, yellow and red LED lights which gives you an indication of how loud the music is and whether you could be distorting the sound. Good mixers will have a separate display for the channel you are cueing, helping you match the volume levels to the one already playing.
Line-in/phono switch	Switches between different pieces of equipment plugged into the same channel such as turntable and CD player. Can also be used to kill the complete sound of a channel allowing you to add dramatic pauses to the music.
Master volume	Controls the level of the overall sound going to the amplifier.
Mic input/mic controls	Allows you or an MC to use a microphone when the music is playing.
Pan	Lets you move a track from one side of the sound system to the other.
Punch/transform buttons	Punches in the sound from the other channel which is useful when scratching.
Samplers	Some models may have a built-in sampler allowing you to create short loops of tracks.
Split cue	Lets you hear a different channel in each ear which is useful if you don't have a monitor speaker or can't hear it very well.

Problems and solutions

Problem	Solution
The crossfader is broken	Use the upfaders to mix instead.
The sound is awful	Ask if there is a sound engineer who can look at the problem. If there isn't, adjust the volume levels making sure the sound levels aren't going into the red. Try turning the master volume on the mixer down whilst compensating by turning the power amps up. It's always best to turn the volume up on the main amp rather than on the mixer if possible. Adjust the EQ levels until things sound rosy.
There is no monitor/the monitor is broken	Use the split-cue button or the headphone mixer and mix using your headphones instead. Or, if there is no split-cue button, see if you can move a speaker closer to the decks so that you can mix off the speaker.
Your headphones break mid-set	Ask to borrow another DJs or failing that get a friend to dash home to get some more. Failing that, start drop mixing.

You stop the wrong record as it's playing to the crowd	Quickly start it again! Or quickly put on a new one as if you meant to do that all along. Don't worry though – all DJs have made this mistake. Learn not to do it again though!
You can't see what you are doing	Always take a small torch such as a Maglite. If that runs out of batteries, use a lighter.
The stylus or cartridge is faulty/broken	Bring a spare or get the manager to swap it. Mix with one turntable and a CD deck if you have to.
There is no sound from one of the channels	Check the faders and gains aren't turned down. Check the line-in/phone switches. Check the phono leads are connected properly.
You are really struggling to keep two records in time	Does one have live drumming in it? This is likely if it was made before the '80s. Deal with it by constantly re-adjusting the tempo. Or use another record.
You are DJing with a laptop and it crashes	The best way to deal with this is to have a back-up machine but even then an embarrassing silence whilst you swap over is unavoidable unless you have some vinyl or CDs at the ready.
The power suddenly stops mid-set	Have you accidentally turned the power switch on the turntable off? Has the amp or mixer failed?
You are getting feedback	Move the decks away from the speakers if you can, or turn down the bass.
There is an annoying electrical humming sound	Your decks aren't earthed properly. Connect the thin single wire coming out of the back of each turntable to the earth screw on the back of the mixer.

The venue manager is giving you grief	Be professional. Don't lose your cool. Politely address the problem if you can.
No one is dancing	Look at what you are playing. Is the music too deep/underground/obscure/loud/quiet? Will changing the musical mood/style help? Will playing a known crowd pleaser be a good idea?
An MC asks you to plug in a mic so he/she can MC over your music	On no account let this happen. It will always sound terrible. Tell them that you don't work with MCs or failing that that there is no microphone or that the microphone channel is not working. If you want to use an MC, use a good MC you know who you have rehearsed with.
You are booked to play a warm-up set but the peak-time DJ doesn't show so you are asked to play the main set	Deal with it. Even if you have only brought warm-up records there will be other mixes/remixes on those records you could get away with playing. Better still, always be prepared by taking a variety of tunes. Better to have too many than too few. DJs using laptops have no excuse. Your entire collection should be on there.
You need to answer nature's call mid-set	Put a long record on and make a dash for it. Do not be tempted to ask a friend or worse still a punter to put the next record on. They will mess it up or even worse start break dancing as they morph into DJ Cliché.

index